AF613204

DELHI

OPEN BOOKS

WORLD WAR 1 POETRY

COLLECTABLE EDITION

WORLD WAR 1 POETRY
COLLECTABLE EDITION
by DELHI OPEN BOOKS

Published by

Delhi Open Books

G/F, 4771/23, Bharat Ram Road, Daryaganj, New Delhi-110002
Ph.: 91-11-42408081
E-mail: delhiopenbooks2016@gmail.com

ISBN: 978-93-90997-27-5

Cover, Typesetting, and Book Design by **ROHIT**

Contents

In Flanders Fields

In Flanders fields the poppies blow
Between the crosses, row on row,
That mark our place; and in the sky
The larks, still bravely singing, fly
Scarce heard amid the guns below.

We are the Dead. Short days ago
We lived, felt dawn, saw sunset glow,
Loved and were loved, and now we lie,
In Flanders fields.

Take up our quarrel with the foe:
To you from failing hands we throw
The torch; be yours to hold it high.
If ye break faith with us who die
We shall not sleep, though poppies grow
In Flanders fields.

The Pilgrims

An uphill path, sun-gleams between the showers,
Where every beam that broke the leaden sky
Lit other hills with fairer ways than ours;
Some clustered graves where half our memories lie;
And one grim Shadow creeping ever nigh:
And this was Life.

Wherein we did another's burden seek,
The tired feet we helped upon the road,
The hand we gave the weary and the weak,
The miles we lightened one another's load,
When, faint to falling, onward yet we strode:
This too was Life.

Till, at the upland, as we turned to go
Amid fair meadows, dusky in the night,
The mists fell back upon the road below;
Broke on our tired eyes the western light;
The very graves were for a moment bright:
And this was Death.

Channel Firing

That night your great guns, unawares,
Shook all our coffins as we lay,
And broke the chancel window-squares,
We thought it was the Judgment-day

And sat upright. While drearisome
Arose the howl of wakened hounds:
The mouse let fall the altar-crumb,
The worms drew back into the mounds,

The glebe cow drooled. Till God called, "No;
It's gunnery practice out at sea
Just as before you went below;
The world is as it used to be:

"All nations striving strong to make
Red war yet redder. Mad as hatters
They do no more for Christés sake
Than you who are helpless in such matters.

"That this is not the judgment-hour
For some of them's a blessed thing,
For if it were they'd have to scour
Hell's floor for so much threatening....

"Ha, ha. It will be warmer when
I blow the trumpet (if indeed
I ever do; for you are men,
And rest eternal sorely need)."

So down we lay again. "I wonder,
Will the world ever saner be,"
Said one, "than when He sent us under
In our indifferent century!"

And many a skeleton shook his head.
"Instead of preaching forty year,"
My neighbour Parson Thirdly said,
"I wish I had stuck to pipes and beer."

Again the guns disturbed the hour,
Roaring their readiness to avenge,
As far inland as Stourton Tower,
And Camelot, and starlit Stonehenge.

On Receiving News of the War

Snow is a strange white word;
No ice or frost
Have asked of bud or bird
For Winter's cost.

Yet ice and frost and snow
From earth to sky
This Summer land doth know,
No man knows why.

In all men's hearts it is.
Some spirit old
Hath turned with malign kiss
Our lives to mould.

Red fangs have torn His face.
God's blood is shed.
He mourns from His lone place
His children dead.

O! ancient crimson curse!
Corrode, consume.
Give back this universe
Its pristine bloom.
(Cape Town, 1914)

Peace

Now, God be thanked who has matched us with his hour,
And caught our youth, and wakened us from sleeping!
With hand made sure, clear eye, and sharpened power,
To turn, as swimmers into cleanness leaping,
Glad from a world grown old and cold and weary;
Leave the sick hearts that honor could not move,
And half-men, and their dirty songs and dreary,
And all the little emptiness of love!
Oh! we, who have known shame, we have found release there,
Where there's no ill, no grief, but sleep has mending,
Naught broken save this body, lost but breath;
Nothing to shake the laughing heart's long peace there,
But only agony, and that has ending;
And the worst friend and enemy is but Death.

The Soldier

If I should die, think only this of me:
That there's some corner of a foreign field
That is for ever England. There shall be
In that rich earth a richer dust concealed;
A dust whom England bore, shaped, made aware,
Gave, once, her flowers to love, her ways to roam;
A body of England's, breathing English air,
Washed by the rivers, blest by suns of home.

And think, this heart, all evil shed away,
A pulse in the eternal mind, no less
Gives somewhere back the thoughts by England given;
Her sights and sounds; dreams happy as her day;
And laughter, learnt of friends; and gentleness,
In hearts at peace, under an English heaven.

The Dead

These hearts were woven of human joys and cares,
Washed marvellously with sorrow, swift to mirth.
The years had given them kindness. Dawn was theirs,
And sunset, and the colours of the earth.
These had seen movement, and heard music; known
Slumber and waking; loved; gone proudly friended;
Felt the quick stir of wonder; sat alone;
Touched flowers and furs and cheeks. All this is ended.

There are waters blown by changing winds to laughter
And lit by the rich skies, all day. And after,
Frost, with a gesture, stays the waves that dance
And wandering loveliness. He leaves a white
Unbroken glory, a gathered radiance,
A width, a shining peace, under the night.

Joining the Colours

There they go marching all in step so gay!
Smooth-cheeked and golden, food for shells and guns.
Blithely they go as to a wedding day,
The mothers' sons.

The drab street stares to see them row on row
On the high tram-tops, singing like the lark.
Too careless-gay for courage, singing they go
Into the dark.

With tin whistles, mouth-organs, any noise,
They pipe the way to glory and the grave;
Foolish and young, the gay and golden boys
Love cannot save.

High heart! High courage! The poor girls they kissed
Run with them : they shall kiss no more, alas!
Out of the mist they stepped-into the mist
Singing they pass.

Men Who March Away

What of the faith and fire within us
Men who march away
Ere the barn-cocks say
Night is growing gray,
Leaving all that here can win us;
What of the faith and fire within us
Men who march away?

Is it a purblind prank, O think you,
Friend with the musing eye,
Who watch us stepping by
With doubt and dolorous sigh?
Can much pondering so hoodwink you!
Is it a purblind prank, O think you,
Friend with the musing eye?

Nay. We well see what we are doing,
Though some may not see—
Dalliers as they be—
England's need are we;
Her distress would leave us rueing:
Nay. We well see what we are doing,
Though some may not see!

In our heart of hearts believing
Victory crowns the just,
And that braggarts must

Surely bite the dust,
Press we to the field ungrieving,
In our heart of hearts believing
Victory crowns the just.

Hence the faith and fire within us
Men who march away
Ere the barn-cocks say
Night is growing gray,
Leaving all that here can win us;
Hence the faith and fire within us
Men who march away.

War Girls

There's the girl who clips your ticket for the train,
And the girl who speeds the lift from floor to floor,
There's the girl who does a milk-round in the rain,
And the girl who calls for orders at your door.
Strong, sensible, and fit,
They're out to show their grit,
And tackle jobs with energy and knack.
No longer caged and penned up,
They're going to keep their end up
Till the khaki soldier boys come marching back.

There's the motor girl who drives a heavy van,
There's the butcher girl who brings your joint of meat,
There's the girl who cries 'All fares, please!' like a man,
And the girl who whistles taxis up the street.
Beneath each uniform
Beats a heart that's soft and warm,
Though of canny mother-wit they show no lack;
But a solemn statement this is,
They've no time for love and kisses
Till the khaki soldier-boys come marching back.

To Germany

You are blind like us. Your hurt no man designed,
And no man claimed the conquest of your land.
But gropers both through fields of thought confined
We stumble and we do not understand.
You only saw your future bigly planned,
And we, the tapering paths of our own mind,
And in each other's dearest ways we stand,
And hiss and hate. And the blind fight the blind.

When it is peace, then we may view again
With new-won eyes each other's truer form
And wonder. Grown more loving-kind and warm
We'll grasp firm hands and laugh at the old pain,
When it is peace. But until peace, the storm
The darkness and the thunder and the rain.

For the Fallen

With proud thanksgiving, a mother for her children,
England mourns for her dead across the sea.
Flesh of her flesh they were, spirit of her spirit,
Fallen in the cause of the free.

Solemn the drums thrill; Death august and royal
Sings sorrow up into immortal spheres,
There is music in the midst of desolation
And a glory that shines upon our tears.

They went with songs to the battle, they were young,
Straight of limb, true of eye, steady and aglow.
They were staunch to the end against odds uncounted;
They fell with their faces to the foe.

They shall grow not old, as we that are left grow old:
Age shall not weary them, nor the years condemn.
At the going down of the sun and in the morning
We will remember them.

They mingle not with their laughing comrades again;
They sit no more at familiar tables of home;
They have no lot in our labour of the day-time;
They sleep beyond England's foam.

But where our desires are and our hopes profound,
Felt as a well-spring that is hidden from sight,
To the innermost heart of their own land they are known
As the stars are known to the Night;

As the stars that shall be bright when we are dust,
Moving in marches upon the heavenly plain;
As the stars that are starry in the time of our darkness,
To the end, to the end, they remain.

Phases

I.

There's a little square in Paris,
Waiting until we pass.
They sit idly there,
They sip the glass.

There's a cab-horse at the corner,
There's rain. The season grieves.
It was silver once,
And green with leaves.

There's a parrot in a window,
Will see us on parade,
Hear the loud drums roll—
And serenade.

II.

This was the salty taste of glory,
That it was not
Like Agamemnon's story.
Only, an eyeball in the mud,
And Hopkins,
Flat and pale and gory!

III.

But the bugles, in the night,
Were wings that bore
To where our comfort was;

Arabesques of candle beams,

Winding
Through our heavy dreams;

Winds that blew
Where the bending iris grew;

Birds of intermitted bliss,
Singing in the night's abyss;
Vines with yellow fruit,
That fell
Along the walls
That bordered Hell.

IV.

Death's nobility again
Beautified the simplest men.
Fallen Winkle felt the pride
Of Agamemnon
When he died.

What could London's
Work and waste
Give him—
To that salty, sacrificial taste?

What could London's
Sorrow bring—
To that short, triumphant sting?

August 1914

The sun rose over the sweep of the hill
All bare for the gathered hay,
And a blackbird sang by the window-sill,
And a girl knelt down to pray:
'Whom Thou hast kept through the night, O Lord,
Keep Thou safe through the day.'

The sun rose over the shell-swept height,
The guns are over the way,
And a soldier turned from the toil of the night
To the toil of another day,
And a bullet sang by the parapet
To drive in the new-turned clay.

The sun sank slow by the sweep of the hill,
They had carried all the hay,
And a blackbird sang by the window-sill,
And a girl knelt down to pray:
'Keep Thou safe through the night, O Lord,
Whom Thou hast kept through the day.'

The sun sank slow by the shell-swept height,
The guns had prepared a way,
And a soldier turned to sleep that night
Who would not wake for the day,
And a blackbird flew from the window-sill,
When a girl knelt down to pray.

August 1914

What in our lives is burnt
In the fire of this?
The heart's dear granary?
The much we shall miss?

Three lives hath one life—
Iron, honey, gold.
The gold, the honey gone—
Left is the hard and cold.

Iron are our lives
Molten right through our youth.
A burnt space through ripe fields,
A fair mouth's broken tooth.

August, 1914

God said, "Men have forgotten Me:
The souls that sleep shall wake again,
And blinded eyes must learn to see."

So since redemption comes through pain
He smote the earth with chastening rod,
And brought destruction's lurid reign;

But where His desolation trod
The people in their agony
Despairing cried, "There is no God.
G.K. Chesterton
Elegy in a Country Churchyard
The men that worked for England
They have their graves at home:
And bees and birds of England
About the cross can roam.

But they that fought for England,
Following a falling star,
Alas, alas for England
They have their graves afar.

And they that rule in England,
In stately conclave met,
Alas, alas for England
They have no graves as yet

Reported Missing

My thought shall never be that you are dead:
Who laughed so lately in this quiet place.
The dear and deep-eyed humour of that face
Held something ever living, in Death's stead.
Scornful I hear the flat things they have said
And all their piteous platitudes of pain.
I laugh! I laugh! – For you will come again –
This heart would never beat if you were dead.
The world's adrowse in twilight hushfulness,
There's purple lilac in your little room,
And somewhere out beyond the evening gloom
Small boys are culling summer watercress.
Of these familiar things I have no dread
Being so very sure you are not dead.

Dulce et Decorum Est

Bent double, like old beggars under sacks,
Knock-kneed, coughing like hags, we cursed through sludge,
Till on the haunting flares we turned our backs
And towards our distant rest began to trudge.
Men marched asleep. Many had lost their boots
But limped on, blood-shod. All went lame; all blind;
Drunk with fatigue; deaf even to the hoots
Of tired, outstripped Five-Nines that dropped behind.
Gas! GAS! Quick, boys! - An ecstasy of fumbling,
Fitting the clumsy helmets just in time;
But someone still was yelling out and stumbling
And flound'ring like a man in fire or lime ...
Dim, through the misty panes and thick green light,
As under I green sea, I saw him drowning.
In all my dreams, before my helpless sight,
He plunges at me, guttering, choking, drowning.
If in some smothering dreams you too could pace
Behind the wagon that we flung him in,
And watch the white eyes writhing in his face,
His hanging face, like a devil's sick of sin;
If you could hear, at every jolt, the blood
Come gargling from the froth-corrupted lungs,
Obscene as cancer, bitter as the cud
Of vile, incurable sores on innocent tongues, --
My friend, you would not tell with such high zest
To children ardent for some desperate glory,
The old lie: Dulce et decorum est
Pro patria mori.

Searchlight

There has been no sound of guns,
No roar of exploding bombs;
But the darkness has an edge
That grits the nerves of the sleeper.
He awakens;
Nothing disturbs the stillness,
Save perhaps the light, slow flap,
Once only, of the curtain
Dim in the darkness.
Yet there is something else
That drags him from his bed;
And he stands in the darkness
With his feet cold against the floor
And the cold air round his ankles.
He does not know why,
But he goes to the window and sees
A beam of light, miles high,
Dividing the night into two before him,
Still, stark and throbbing.
The houses and gardens beneath
Lie under the snow
Quiet and tinged with purple.
There has been no sound of guns,
No roar of exploding bombs;
Only that watchfulness hidden among
the snow-covered houses,
And that great beam thrusting back into heaven
The light taken from it.

Easter Monday
(In memoriam E.T.)

In the last letter that I had from France
You thanked me for the silver Easter egg
Which I had hidden in the box of apples
You liked to munch beyond all other fruit.
You found the egg the Monday before Easter,
And said, 'I will praise Easter Monday now –
It was such a lovely morning'. Then you spoke
Of the coming battle and said, 'This is the eve.
Good-bye. And may I have a letter soon.'
That Easter Monday was a day for praise,
It was such a lovely morning. In our garden
We sowed our earliest seeds, and in the orchard
The apple-bud was ripe. It was the eve.
There are three letters that you will not get.

To His Love

He's gone, and all our plans
Are useless indeed.
We'll walk no more on Cotswold
Where the sheep feed
Quietly and take no heed.
His body that was so quick
Is not as you
Knew it, on Severn river
Under the blue
Driving our small boat through.
You would not know him now . . .
But still he died
Nobly, so cover him over
With violets of pride
Purple from Severn side.
Cover him, cover him soon!
And with thick-set
Masses of memoried flowers—
Hide that red wet
Thing I must somehow forget.

Break of Day in the Trenches

The darkness crumbles away.
It is the same old druid Time as ever,
Only a live thing leaps my hand,
A queer sardonic rat,
As I pull the parapet's poppy
To stick behind my ear.
Droll rat, they would shoot you if they knew
Your cosmopolitan sympathies.
Now you have touched this English hand
You will do the same to a German
Soon, no doubt, if it be your pleasure
To cross the sleeping green between.
It seems you inwardly grin as you pass
Strong eyes, fine limbs, haughty athletes,
Less chanced than you for life,
Bonds to the whims of murder,
Sprawled in the bowels of the earth,
The torn fields of France.
What do you see in our eyes
At the shrieking iron and flame
Hurled through still heavens?
What quaver — what heart aghast?
Poppies whose roots are in man's veins
Drop, and are ever dropping;
But mine in my ear is safe —
Just a little white with the dust.

The Lament of the Demobilized

'Four years,' some say consolingly. 'Oh well,
What's that? You're young. And then it must have been
A very fine experience for you!'
And they forget
How others stayed behind and just got on—
Got on the better since we were away.
And we came home and found
They had achieved, and men revered their names,
But never mentioned ours;
And no one talked heroics now, and we
Must just go back and start again once more.
'You threw four years into the melting-pot—
Did you indeed!' these others cry. 'Oh well,
The more fool you!'
And we're beginning to agree with them.

Reconciliation

When you are standing at your hero's grave,
Or near some homeless village where he died,
Remember, through your heart's rekindling pride,
The German soldiers who were loyal and brave.
Men fought like brutes; and hideous things were done,
And you have nourished hatred harsh and blind.
But in that Golgotha perhaps you'll find
The mothers of the men who killed your son.

An Irish Airman Foresees His Death

I know that I shall meet my fate
Somewhere among the clouds above;
Those that I fight I do not hate,
Those that I guard I do not love;
My country is Kiltartan Cross,
My countrymen Kiltartan's poor,
No likely end could bring them loss
Or leave them happier than before.
Nor law, nor duty bade me fight,
Nor public men, nor cheering crowds,
A lonely impulse of delight
Drove to this tumult in the clouds;
I balanced all, brought all to mind,
The years to come seemed waste of breath,
A waste of breath the years behind
In balance with this life, this death.

As the Team's Head Brass

As the team's head brass flashed out on the turn
The lovers disappeared into the wood.
I sat among the boughs of the fallen elm
That strewed an angle of the fallow, and
Watched the plough narrowing a yellow square
Of charlock. Every time the horses turned
Instead of treading me down, the ploughman leaned
Upon the handles to say or ask a word,
About the weather, next about the war.
Scraping the share he faced towards the wood,
And screwed along the furrow
till the brass flashedOnce more.
The blizzard felled the elm whose crest
I sat in, by a woodpecker's round hole,
The ploughman said. 'When will they take it away?'
'When the war's over.' So the talk began—
One minute and an interval of ten,
A minute more and the same interval.
'Have you been out?' 'No.' 'And don't want to, perhaps?'
'If I could only come back again, I should.
I could spare an arm. I shouldn't want to lose
A leg. If I should lose my head, why, so,
I should want nothing more. . . . Have many gone
From here?' 'Yes.' 'Many lost?' 'Yes, a good few.
Only two teams work on the farm this year.
One of my mates is dead. The second day
In France they killed him. It was back in March,
The very night of the blizzard, too. Now if
He had stayed here we should have moved the tree.'

'And I should not have sat here. Everything
Would have been different. For it would have been
Another world.' 'Ay, and a better, though
If we could see all all might seem good.' Then
The lovers came out of the wood again:
The horses started and for the last time
I watched the clods crumble and topple over
After the ploughshare and the stumbling team.

Anthem for Doomed Youth

What passing-bells for these who die as cattle?
— Only the monstrous anger of the guns.
Only the stuttering rifles' rapid rattle
Can patter out their hasty orisons.
No mockeries now for them; no prayers nor bells;
Nor any voice of mourning save the choirs,—
The shrill, demented choirs of wailing shells;
And bugles calling for them from sad shires.

What candles may be held to speed them all?
Not in the hands of boys, but in their eyes
Shall shine the holy glimmers of goodbyes.
The pallor of girls' brows shall be their pall;
Their flowers the tenderness of patient minds,
And each slow dusk a drawing-down of blinds.

Arms and the Boy

Let the boy try along this bayonet-blade
How cold steel is, and keen with hunger of blood;
Blue with all malice, like a madman's flash;
And thinly drawn with famishing for flesh.

Lend him to stroke these blind, blunt bullet-leads,
Which long to nuzzle in the hearts of lads,
Or give him cartridges of fine zinc teeth
Sharp with the sharpness of grief and death.

For his teeth seem for laughing round an apple.
There lurk no claws behind his fingers supple;
And God will grow no talons at his heels,
Nor antlers through the thickness of his curls.

Disabled

He sat in a wheeled chair, waiting for dark,
And shivered in his ghastly suit of grey,
Legless, sewn short at elbow. Through the park
Voices of boys rang saddening like a hymn,
Voices of play and pleasure after day,
Till gathering sleep had mothered them from him.

* * * * *

About this time Town used to swing so gay
When glow-lamps budded in the light-blue trees,
And girls glanced lovelier as the air grew dim,—
In the old times, before he threw away his knees.
Now he will never feel again how slim
Girls' waists are, or how warm their subtle hands,
All of them touch him like some queer disease.

* * * * *

There was an artist silly for his face,
For it was younger than his youth, last year.
Now, he is old; his back will never brace;
He's lost his colour very far from here,
Poured it down shell-holes till the veins ran dry,
And half his lifetime lapsed in the hot race
And leap of purple spurted from his thigh.

* * * * *

One time he liked a blood-smear down his leg,
After the matches carried shoulder-high.

It was after football, when he'd drunk a peg,
He thought he'd better join. He wonders why.
Someone had said he'd look a god in kilts.
That's why; and maybe, too, to please his Meg,
Aye, that was it, to please the giddy jilts,
He asked to join. He didn't have to beg;
Smiling they wrote his lie: aged nineteen years.
Germans he scarcely thought of, all their guilt,
And Austria's, did not move him. And no fears
Of Fear came yet. He thought of jewelled hilts
For daggers in plaid socks; of smart salutes;
And care of arms; and leave; and pay arrears;
Esprit de corps; and hints for young recruits.
And soon, he was drafted out with drums and cheers.

* * * * *

Some cheered him home, but not as crowds cheer Goal.
Only a solemn man who brought him fruits
Thanked him; and then inquired about his soul.

* * * * *

Now, he will spend a few sick years in institutes,
And do what things the rules consider wise,
And take whatever pity they may dole.
Tonight he noticed how the women's eyes
Passed from him to the strong men that were whole.
How cold and late it is! Why don't they come
And put him into bed? Why don't they come?

Exposure

Our brains ache, in the merciless iced east winds that knive
us...
Wearied we keep awake because the night is silent...
Low drooping flares confuse our memory of the salient...
Worried by silence, sentries whisper, curious, nervous,
But nothing happens.

Watching, we hear the mad gusts tugging on the wire,
Like twitching agonies of men among its brambles.
Northward, incessantly, the flickering gunnery rumbles,
Far off, like a dull rumour of some other war.
What are we doing here?

The poignant misery of dawn begins to grow...
We only know war lasts, rain soaks, and clouds sag stormy.
Dawn massing in the east her melancholy army
Attacks once more in ranks on shivering ranks of grey,
But nothing happens.

Sudden successive flights of bullets streak the silence.
Less deadly than the air that shudders black with snow,
With sidelong flowing flakes that flock, pause, and renew,
We watch them wandering up
and down the wind's nonchalance,
But nothing happens.

Pale flakes with fingering stealth come feeling for our faces—
We cringe in holes, back on forgotten dreams, and stare,
snow-dazed,

Deep into grassier ditches. So we drowse, sun-dozed,
Littered with blossoms trickling where the blackbird fusses.
—Is it that we are dying?

Slowly our ghosts drag home: glimpsing the sunk fires, glozed
With crusted dark-red jewels; crickets jingle there;
For hours the innocent mice rejoice: the house is theirs;
Shutters and doors, all closed: on us the doors are closed,—
We turn back to our dying.

Since we believe not otherwise can kind fires burn;
Now ever suns smile true on child, or field, or fruit.
For God's invincible spring our love is made afraid;
Therefore, not loath, we lie out here; therefore were born,
For love of God seems dying.

Tonight, this frost will fasten on this mud and us,
Shrivelling many hands, and puckering foreheads crisp.
The burying-party, picks and shovels in shaking grasp,
Pause over half-known faces. All their eyes are ice,
But nothing happens.

Futility

Move him into the sun—
Gently its touch awoke him once,
At home, whispering of fields half-sown.
Always it woke him, even in France,
Until this morning and this snow.
If anything might rouse him now
The kind old sun will know.

Think how it wakes the seeds—
Woke once the clays of a cold star.
Are limbs, so dear-achieved, are sides
Full-nerved, still warm, too hard to stir?
Was it for this the clay grew tall?
—O what made fatuous sunbeams toil
To break earth's sleep at all?

Absolution

The anguish of the earth absolves our eyes
Till beauty shines in all that we can see.
War is our scourge; yet war has made us wise,
And, fighting for our freedom, we are free.

Horror of wounds and anger at the foe,
And loss of things desired; all these must pass.
We are the happy legion, for we know
Time's but a golden wind that shakes the grass.

There was an hour when we were loth to part
From life we longed to share no less than others.
Now, having claimed this heritage of heart,
What need we more, my comrades and my brothers?

Counter-Attack

We'd gained our first objective hours before
While dawn broke like a face with blinking eyes,
Pallid, unshaven and thirsty, blind with smoke.
Things seemed all right at first. We held their line,
With bombers posted, Lewis guns well placed,
And clink of shovels deepening the shallow trench.
The place was rotten with dead; green clumsy legs
High-booted, sprawled and grovelled along the saps
And trunks, face downward, in the sucking mud,
Wallowed like trodden sand-bags loosely filled;
And naked sodden buttocks, mats of hair,
Bulged, clotted heads slept in the plastering slime.
And then the rain began,—the jolly old rain!

A yawning soldier knelt against the bank,
Staring across the morning blear with fog;
He wondered when the Allemands would get busy;
And then, of course, they started with five-nines
Traversing, sure as fate, and never a dud.
Mute in the clamour of shells he watched them burst
Spouting dark earth and wire with gusts from hell,
While posturing giants dissolved in drifts of smoke.
He crouched and flinched, dizzy with galloping fear,
Sick for escape,—loathing the strangled horror
And butchered, frantic gestures of the dead.

An officer came blundering down the trench:
"Stand-to and man the fire step!" On he went ...
Gasping and bawling, "Fire-step ... counter-attack!"

Then the haze lifted. Bombing on the right
Down the old sap: machine-guns on the left;
And stumbling figures looming out in front.
"O Christ, they're coming at us!" Bullets spat,
And he remembered his rifle ... rapid fire ...
And started blazing wildly ... then a bang
Crumpled and spun him sideways, knocked him out
To grunt and wriggle: none heeded him; he choked
And fought the flapping veils of smothering gloom,
Lost in a blurred confusion of yells and groans ...
Down, and down, and down, he sank and drowned,
Bleeding to death. The counter-attack had failed.

The Death Bed

He drowsed and was aware of silence heaped
Round him, unshaken as the steadfast walls;
Aqueous like floating rays of amber light,
Soaring and quivering in the wings of sleep.
Silence and safety; and his mortal shore
Lipped by the inward, moonless waves of death.

Someone was holding water to his mouth.
He swallowed, unresisting; moaned and dropped
Through crimson gloom to darkness; and forgot
The opiate throb and ache that was his wound.
Water—calm, sliding green above the weir;
Water—a sky-lit alley for his boat,
Bird-voiced, and bordered with reflected flowers
And shaken hues of summer: drifting down,
He dipped contented oars, and sighed, and slept.

Night, with a gust of wind, was in the ward,
Blowing the curtain to a gummering curve.
Night. He was blind; he could not see the stars
Glinting among the wraiths of wandering cloud;
Queer blots of colour, purple, scarlet, green,
Flickered and faded in his drowning eyes.

Rain—he could hear it rustling through the dark;
Fragrance and passionless music woven as one;
Warm rain on drooping roses; pattering showers
That soak the woods; not the harsh rain that sweeps
Behind the thunder, but a trickling peace,

Gently and slowly washing life away.

He stirred, shifting his body; then the pain
Leaped like a prowling beast, and gripped and tore
His groping dreams with grinding claws and fangs.
But someone was beside him; soon he lay
Shuddering because that evil thing had passed.
And death, who'd stepped toward him, paused and stared.

Light many lamps and gather round his bed.
Lend him your eyes, warm blood, and will to live.
Speak to him; rouse him; you may save him yet.
He's young; he hated war; how should he die
When cruel old campaigners win safe through?

But death replied: "I choose him." So he went,
And there was silence in the summer night;
Silence and safety; and the veils of sleep.
Then, far away, the thudding of the guns.

The General

“Good-morning, good-morning!” the General said
When we met him last week on our way to the line.
Now the soldiers he smiled at are most of ‘em dead,
And we’re cursing his staff for incompetent swine.
“He’s a cheery old card,” grunted Harry to Jack
As they slogged up to Arras with rifle and pack.

But he did for them both by his plan of attack.

Glory of Women

You love us when we're heroes, home on leave,
Or wounded in a mentionable place.
You worship decorations; you believe
That chivalry redeems the war's disgrace.
You make us shells. You listen with delight,
By tales of dirt and danger fondly thrilled.
You crown our distant ardours while we fight,
And mourn our laurelled memories when we're killed.
You can't believe that British troops "retire"
When hell's last horror breaks them, and they run,
Trampling the terrible corpses—blind with blood.
O German mother dreaming by the fire,
While you are knitting socks to send your son
His face is trodden deeper in the mud.

Break of Day in the Trenches

The darkness crumbles away.
It is the same old druid Time as ever,
Only a live thing leaps my hand,
A queer sardonic rat,
As I pull the parapet's poppy
To stick behind my ear.
Droll rat, they would shoot you if they knew
Your cosmopolitan sympathies.
Now you have touched this English hand
You will do the same to a German
Soon, no doubt, if it be your pleasure
To cross the sleeping green between.
It seems you inwardly grin as you pass
Strong eyes, fine limbs, haughty athletes,
Less chanced than you for life,
Bonds to the whims of murder,
Sprawled in the bowels of the earth,
The torn fields of France.
What do you see in our eyes
At the shrieking iron and flame
Hurled through still heavens?
What quaver—what heart aghast?
Poppies whose roots are in man's veins
Drop, and are ever dropping;
But mine in my ear is safe—
Just a little white with the dust.

The Troop Ship

Grotesque and queerly huddled
Contortionists to twist
The sleepy soul to a sleep,
We lie all sorts of ways
And cannot sleep.
The wet wind is so cold,
And the lurching men so careless,
That, should you drop to a doze,
Wind's fumble or men's feet
Is on your face.

The Kiss

To these I turn, in these I trust—
Brother Lead and Sister Steel.
To his blind power I make appeal,
I guard her beauty clean from rust.

He spins and burns and loves the air,
And splits a skull to win my praise;
But up the nobly marching days
She glitters naked, cold and fair.

Sweet Sister, grant your soldier this:
That in good fury he may feel
The body where he sets his heel
Quail from your downward darting kiss.

Sonnet 9 : On Returning to the Front after Leave

Apart sweet women (for whom Heaven be blessed),
Comrades, you cannot think how thin and blue

Look the leftovers of mankind that rest,
Now that the cream has been skimmed off in you.
War has its horrors, but has this of good—
That its sure processes sort out and bind
Brave hearts in one intrepid brotherhood
And leave the shams and imbeciles behind.
Now turn we joyful to the great attacks,
Not only that we face in a fair field
Our valiant foe and all his deadly tools,
But also that we turn disdainful backs
On that poor world we scorn yet die to shield—
That world of cowards, hypocrites, and fools.

The War Films

O living pictures of the dead,
O songs without a sound,
O fellowship whose phantom tread
Hallows a phantom ground—
How in a gleam have these revealed
The faith we had not found.

We have sought God in a cloudy Heaven,
We have passed by God on earth:
His seven sins and his sorrows seven,
His wayworn mood and mirth,
Like a ragged cloak have hid from us
The secret of his birth.

Brother of men, when now I see
The lads go forth in line,
Thou knowest my heart is hungry in me
As for thy bread and wine;
Thou knowest my heart is bowed in me
To take their death for mine.

The Night Patrol

France, March 1916.
Over the top! The wire's thin here, unbarbed
Plain rusty coils, not staked, and low enough:
Full of old tins, though—"When you're through, all three,
Aim quarter left for fifty yards or so,
Then straight for that new piece of German wire;
See if it's thick, and listen for a while
For sounds of working; don't run any risks;
About an hour; now, over!"
And we placed
Our hands on the topmost sand-bags, leapt, and stood
A second with curved backs, then crept to the wire,
Wormed ourselves tinkling through,
glanced back, and dropped.
The sodden ground was splashed with shallow pools,
And tufts of crackling cornstalks, two years old,
No man had reaped, and patches of spring grass.
Half-seen, as rose and sank the flares, were strewn
The wrecks of our attack: the bandoliers,
Packs, rifles, bayonets, belts, and haversacks,
Shell fragments, and the huge whole forms of shells
Shot fruitlessly—and everywhere the dead.
Only the dead were always present—present
As a vile sickly smell of rottenness;
The rustling stubble and the early grass,
The slimy pools — the dead men stank through all,
Pungent and sharp; as bodies loomed before,
And as we passed, they stank: then dulled away
To that vague fœtor, all encompassing,

Infecting earth and air. They lay, all clothed,
Each in some new and piteous attitude
That we well marked to guide us back: as he,
Outside our wire, that lay on his back and crossed
His legs Crusader-wise: I smiled at that,
And thought on Elia and his Temple Church.
From him, at quarter left, lay a small corpse,
Down in a hollow, huddled as in a bed,
That one of us put his hand on unawares.
Next was a bunch of half a dozen men
All blown to bits, an archipelago
Of corrupt fragments, vexing to us three,
Who had no light to see by, save the flares.
On such a trail, so light, for ninety yards
We crawled on belly and elbows, till we saw,
Instead of lumpish dead before our eyes,
The stakes and crosslines of the German wire.
We lay in shelter of the last dead man,
Ourselves as dead, and heard their shovels ring
Turning the earth, then talk and cough at times.
A sentry fired and a machine-gun spat;
They shot a glare above us, when it fell
And spluttered out in the pools of No Man's Land,
We turned and crawled past the remembered dead:
Past him and him, and them and him, until,
For he lay some way apart, we caught the scent
Of the Crusader and slide past his legs,
And through the wire and home, and got our rum.

Ode in Memory of the American Volunteers Fallen for France

(To have been read before the statue of Lafayette and Washington in Paris, on Decoration Day, May 30, 1916)

I

Ay, it is fitting on this holiday,
Commemorative of our soldier dead,
When—with sweet flowers of our New England May
Hiding the lichened stones by fifty years made gray—
Their graves in every town are garlanded,
That pious tribute should be given too
To our intrepid few
Obscurely fallen here beyond their seas.
Those to preserve their country's greatness died;
But by the death of these
Something that we can look upon with pride
Has been achieved, nor wholly unreplied
Can sneerers triumph in the charge they make
That from a war where Freedom was at stake
America withheld and, daunted, stood aside.

II

Be they remembered here with each reviving spring,
Not only that in May, when life is loveliest,
Around Neuville-Saint-Vaast and the disputed crest
Of Vimy, they, superb, unfaltering,
In that fine onslaught that no fire could halt,
Parted impetuous to their first assault;
But that they brought fresh hearts and springlike too

To that high mission, and 'tis meet to strew
With twigs of lilac and spring's earliest rose
The cenotaph of those
Who in the cause that history most endears
Fell in the sunny morn and flower of their young years.

III

Yet sought they neither recompense nor praise,
Nor to be mentioned in another breath
Than their blue-coated comrades whose great days
It was their pride to share—ay, share even to the death!
Nay, rather, France, to you they rendered thanks
(Seeing they came for honour, not for gain),
Who, opening to them your glorious ranks,
Gave them that grand occasion to excel,
That chance to live the life most free from stain
And that rare privilege of dying well.

IV

O friends! I know not since that war began
From which no people nobly stands aloof
If in all moments we have given proof
Of virtues that were thought American.
I know not if in all things done and said
All has been well and good,
Or of each one of us can hold his head
As proudly as he should,
Or, from the pattern of those mighty dead
Whose shades our country venerates to-day,
If we 've not somewhat fallen and somewhat gone astray,
But you to whom our land's good name is dear,
If there be any here
Who wonder if her manhood be decreased,
Relaxed its sinews and its blood less red

Than that at Shiloh and Antietam shed,
Be proud of these, have joy in this at least,
And cry: Now heaven be praised
That in that hour that most imperilled her,
Menaced her liberty who foremost raised
Europe's bright flag of freedom, some there were
Who, not unmindful of the antique debt,
Came back the generous path of Lafayette;
And when of a most formidable foe
She checked each onset, arduous to stem—
Foiled and frustrated them—
On those red fields where blow with furious blow
Was countered, whether the gigantic fray
Rolled by the Meuse or at the Bois Sabot,
Accents of ours were in the fierce mêlée;
And on those furthest rims of hallowed ground
Where the forlorn, the gallant charge expires,
When the slain bugler has long ceased to sound,
And on the tangled wires
The last wild rally staggers, crumbles, stops,
Withered beneath the shrapnel's iron showers:—
Now heaven be thanked, we gave a few brave drops;
Now heaven be thanked, a few brave drops were ours.'

V

There, holding still, in frozen steadfastness,
Their bayonets toward the beckoning frontiers,
They lie—our comrades—lie among their peers,
Clad in the glory of fallen warriors,
Grim clustered under thorny trellises,
Dry, furthest foam upon disastrous shores,
Leaves that made last year beautiful, still strewn
Even as they fell, unchanged, beneath the changing moon;
And earth in her divine indifference

Rolls on, and many paltry things and mean
Prate to be heard and caper to be seen.
But they are silent, clam; their eloquence
Is that incomparable attitude;
No human presences their witness are,
But summer clouds and sunset crimson-hued,
And showers and night winds and the northern star
Nay, even our salutations seem profane,
Opposed to their Elysian quietude;
Our salutations calling from afar,
From our ignobler plane
And undistinction of our lesser parts:
Hail, brothers, and farewell; you are twice blest, brave hearts.
Double your glory is who perished thus,
For you have died for France and vindicated us.

At the Movies

They swing across the screen in brave array,
Long British columns grinding the dark grass.
Twelve months ago they marched into the grey
Of battle; yet again behold them pass!

One lifts his dusty cap; his hair is bright;
I meet his eyes, eager and young and bold.
The picture quivers into ghostly white;
Then I remember, and my heart grows cold!

Two Fusiliers

And have we done with War at last?
Well, we've been lucky devils both,
And there's no need of pledge or oath
To bind our lovely friendship fast,
By firmer stuff
Close bound enough.

By wire and wood and stake we're bound,
By Fricourt and by Festubert,
By whipping rain, by the sun's glare,
By all the misery and loud sound,
By a Spring day,
By Picard clay.

Show me the two so closely bound
As we, by the wet bond of blood,
By friendship blossoming from mud,
By Death: we faced him, and we found
Beauty in Death,
In dead men, breath.

from At the Somme: The Song of the Mud

This is the song of the mud,
The pale yellow glistening mud that covers the hills like satin;
The grey gleaming silvery mud that is spread like enamel over the valleys;
The frothing, squirting, spurting, liquid mud that gurgles along the road beds;
The thick elastic mud that is kneaded and pounded and squeezed under the hoofs of the horses;
The invincible, inexhaustible mud of the war zone.

This is the song of the mud, the uniform of the poilu.
His coat is of mud, his great dragging flapping coat, that is too big for him and too heavy;
His coat that once was blue and now is grey and stiff with the mud that cakes to it.
This is the mud that clothes him.
His trousers and boots are of mud,
And his skin is of mud;
And there is mud in his beard.
His head is crowned with a helmet of mud.
He wears it well.
He wears it as a king wears the ermine that bores him.
He has set a new style in clothing;
He has introduced the chic of mud.

This is the song of the mud that wriggles its way into battle.
The impertinent, the intrusive,
the ubiquitous, the unwelcome,

The slimy inveterate nuisance,
That fills the trenches,
That mixes in with the food of the soldiers,
That spoils the working of motors
and crawls into their secret parts,
That spreads itself over the guns,
That sucks the guns down and holds them fast in its slimy
voluminous lips,
That has no respect for destruction and muzzles
the bursting shells;
And slowly, softly, easily,
Soaks up the fire, the noise; soaks up
the energy and the courage;
Soaks up the power of armies;
Soaks up the battle.
Just soaks it up and thus stops it.

This is the hymn of mud-the obscene, the filthy, the putrid,
The vast liquid grave of our armies. It has drowned our men.
Its monstrous distended belly reeks with the undigested dead.
Our men have gone into it, sinking slowly,
and struggling and slowly disappearing.
Our fine men, our brave, strong, young men;
Our glowing red, shouting, brawny men.
Slowly, inch by inch, they have gone down into it,
Into its darkness, its thickness, its silence.
Slowly, irresistibly, it drew them down, sucked them down,
And they were drowned in thick, bitter, heaving mud.
Now it hides them, Oh, so many of them!
Under its smooth glistening surface it is hiding them blandly.
There is not a trace of them.
There is no mark where they went down.
The mute enormous mouth of
the mud has closed over them.

This is the song of the mud,
The beautiful glistening golden mud
that covers the hills like satin;
The mysterious gleaming silvery mud
that is spread like enamel over the valleys.
Mud, the disguise of the war zone;
Mud, the mantle of battles;
Mud, the smooth fluid grave of our soldiers:
This is the song of the mud.

The Dead Kings

All the dead kings came to me
At Rosnaree, where I was dreaming,
A few stars glimmered through the morn,
And down the thorn the dews were streaming.

And every dead king had a story
Of ancient glory, sweetly told.
It was too early for the lark,
But the starry dark had tints of gold.

I listened to the sorrows three
Of that Eire passed into song.
A cock crowed near a hazel croft,
And up aloft dim larks winged strong.

And I, too, told the kings a story
Of later glory, her fourth sorrow:
There was a sound like moving shields
In high green fields and the lowland furrow.

And one said: 'We who yet are kings
Have heard these things lamenting inly.'
Sweet music flowed from many a bill
And on the hill the morn stood queenly.

And one said: 'Over is the singing,
And bell bough ringing, whence we come;
With heavy hearts we'll tread the shadows,
In honey meadows birds are dumb.'

And one said: 'Since the poets perished
And all they cherished in the way,
Their thoughts unsung, like petal showers
Inflame the hours of blue and grey.'

And one said: 'A loud tramp of men
We'll hear again at Rosnaree.'
A bomb burst near me where I lay.
I woke, 'twas day in Picardy.

Servitude

If it were not for England, who would bear
This heavy servitude one moment more?
To keep a brothel, sweep and wash the floor
Of filthiest hovels were noble to compare
With this brass-cleaning life. Now here, now there
Harried in foolishness, scanned curiously o'er
By fools made brazen by conceit, and store
Of antique witticisms thin and bare.

Only the love of comrades sweetens all,
Whose laughing spirit will not be outdone.
As night-watching men wait for the sun
To hearten them, so wait I on such boys
As neither brass nor Hell-fire may appal,
Nor guns, nor sergeant-major's bluster and noise.

Dead Man's Dump

The plunging limbers over the shattered track
Racketed with their rusty freight,
Stuck out like many crowns of thorns,
And the rusty stakes like sceptres old
To stay the flood of brutish men
Upon our brothers dear.

The wheels lurched over sprawled dead
But pained them not, though their bones crunched,
Their shut mouths made no moan.
They lie there huddled, friend and foeman,
Man born of man, and born of woman,
And shells go crying over them
From night till night and now.

Earth has waited for them,
All the time of their growth
Fretting for their decay:
Now she has them at last!
In the strength of their strength
Suspended—stopped and held.

What fierce imaginings their dark souls lit?
Earth! have they gone into you!
Somewhere they must have gone,
And flung on your hard back
Is their soul's sack
Emptied of God-ancestralled essences.
Who hurled them out? Who hurled?

None saw their spirits' shadow shake the grass,
Or stood aside for the half used life to pass
Out of those doomed nostrils and the doomed mouth,
When the swift iron burning bee
Drained the wild honey of their youth.

What of us who, flung on the shrieking pyre,
Walk, our usual thoughts untouched,
Our lucky limbs as on ichor fed,
Immortal seeming ever?
Perhaps when the flames beat loud on us,
A fear may choke in our veins
And the startled blood may stop.

The air is loud with death,
The dark air spurts with fire,
The explosions ceaseless are.
Timelessly now, some minutes past,
Those dead strode time with vigorous life,
Till the shrapnel called 'An end!'
But not to all. In bleeding pangs
Some borne on stretchers dreamed of home,
Dear things, war-blotted from their hearts.

Maniac Earth! howling and flying, your bowel
Seared by the jagged fire, the iron love,
The impetuous storm of savage love.
Dark Earth! dark Heavens! swinging in chemic smoke,
What dead are born when you kiss each soundless soul
With lightning and thunder from your mined heart,
Which man's self dug, and his blind fingers loosed?

A man's brains splattered on
A stretcher-bearer's face;

His shook shoulders slipped their load,
But when they bent to look again
The drowning soul was sunk too deep
For human tenderness.

They left this dead with the older dead,
Stretched at the cross roads.

Burnt black by strange decay
Their sinister faces lie,
The lid over each eye,
The grass and coloured clay
More motion have than they,
Joined to the great sunk silences.

Here is one not long dead;
His dark hearing caught our far wheels,
And the choked soul stretched weak hands
To reach the living word the far wheels said,
The blood-dazed intelligence beating for light,
Crying through the suspense of the far torturing wheels
Swift for the end to break
Or the wheels to break,
Cried as the tide of the world broke over his sight.

Will they come? Will they ever come?
Even as the mixed hoofs of the mules,
The quivering-bellied mules,
And the rushing wheels all mixed
With his tortured upturned sight.
So we crashed round the bend,
We heard his weak scream,
We heard his very last sound,
And our wheels grazed his dead face.

Sergeant-Major Money

It wasn't our battalion, but we lay alongside it,
So the story is as true as the telling is frank.
They hadn't one Line-officer left, after Arras,
Except a batty major and the Colonel, who drank.

'B' Company Commander was fresh from the Depot,
An expert on gas drill, otherwise a dud;
So Sergeant-Major Money carried on, as instructed,
And that's where the swaddies began to sweat blood.

His Old Army humour was so well-spiced and hearty
That one poor sod shot himself, and one lost his wits;
But discipline's maintained, and back in rest-billets
The Colonel congratulates 'B' Company on their kits.

The subalterns went easy, as was only natural
With a terror like Money driving the machine,
Till finally two Welshmen, butties from the Rhondda,
Bayoneted their bugbear in a field-canteen.

Well, we couldn't blame the officers, they relied on Money;
We couldn't blame the pitboys, their courage was grand;
Or, least of all, blame Money, an old stiff surviving
In a New (bloody) Army he couldn't understand.

from The Work

Not fierce and tender but sweet.
This is our impression of the soldiers.
We call our machine Aunt Pauline.
Fasten it fat, that is us, we say Aunt Pauline.
When we left Paris we had rain.
Not snow now nor that in between.
We did have snow then.
Now we are bold.
We are accustomed to it.
All the weights are measures.
By this we mean we know how much oil we use for the machine.

* * *

Hurrah for America.
Here we met a Captain and take him part way.
A day's sun.
Is this Miss.
Yes indeed our mat.
We meant by this that we were always meeting people and that it was pleasant.
We can thank you.
We thank you.
Soldiers of course spoke to us.
Come together.
Come to me there now.
They read on our van American Committee in aid of French wounded.
All of it is bit.

Bitter.This is the way they say we do help.
In the meaning of bright.
Bright not light.
This comforts them when they speak to me. I often discuss America with them and what we hope to do. They listen well and say we hope so too.
We all do.

* * *

This is apropros of the birthplace of Maréchal Joffre. We visited it and we have sent postal cards of it.
The committee will be pleased.
It is not a bother to be a soldier.
I think kindly of that bother.
Can you say lapse.
Then think about it.
Indeed it is yet.
We are so pleased.
With the flag.
With the flag of sets.
Sets of color.
Do you like flags.
Blue flags smell sweetly.
Blue flags in a whirl.
We did this we had ribbon of the American flag and we cut it up and we gave each soldier one with a pin and they pinned it on and we were pleased and we received a charming letter from a telephonist at the front who heard from a friend in Perpignan that we were giving this bit of ribbon and he asked for some and we sent them and we hope
that they are all living.
The wind blows.
And the automobile goes.
Can you guess boards.

Wood.
Naturally we think about wind because this country of Rousillon is the windiest corner in France. Also it is a great wine country.

*   *   *

This is apropos of the fact that I always ask where they come from and then I am ashamed to say I don't know all the Departments but I am learning them.
In the meantime.
In the meantime we are useful.
That is what I mean to say.
In the meantime can you have beds. This means that knowing the number
of beds you begin to know the hospital.
Kindly call a brother.
What is a cure.
I speak french.
What one means.
I can call it in time.
By the way where are fish.
They all love fishing.
In that case are there any wonders.
Many wonders are women.
I could almost say that that was apropos of
my cranking my machine.
And men too.
We smile.
In the way sentences.
He does not feel as we do.
But he did have the coat.
He blushed a little.
This is sometimes when they can't quite help themselves and

they want to help us.
We do not understand the weather. That astonishes me.
Camellias in Perpignan.
Camellias finish when roses begin.
Thank you in smiles.
In this way we go on. So far we have had no troubles yet and yet we do need material.
It is astonishing that those who have fought so hard and so well should pick yellow irises and fish in a stream.
And then a pansy.
I did not ask for it.
It smells.
A sweet smell.
With acacia.
Call it locusts.
Call it me.
I finish by saying that the french soldier is the person we should all help.

After the War

After the war perhaps I'll sit again
Out on the terrace where I sat with you,
And see the changeless sky and hills beat blue
And live an afternoon of summer through.

I shall remember then, and sad at heart
For the lost day of happiness we knew,
Wish only that some other man were you
And spoke my name as once you used to do.

To Any Dead Officer

Well, how are things in Heaven? I wish you'd say,
Because I'd like to know that you're all right.
Tell me, have you found everlasting day,
Or been sucked in by everlasting night?
For when I shut my eyes your face shows plain;
I hear you make some cheery old remark—
I can rebuild you in my brain,
Though you've gone out patrolling in the dark.

You hated tours of trenches; you were proud
Of nothing more than having good years to spend;
Longed to get home and join the careless crowd
Of chaps who work in peace with Time for friend.
That's all washed out now. You're beyond the wire:
No earthly chance can send you crawling back;
You've finished with machine-gun fire—
Knocked over in a hopeless dud-attack.

Somehow I always thought you'd get done in,
Because you were so desperate keen to live:
You were all out to try and save your skin,
Well knowing how much the world had got to give.
You joked at shells and talked the usual "shop,"
Stuck to your dirty job and did it fine:
With "Jesus Christ! when will it stop?
Three years ... It's hell unless we break their line."

So when they told me you'd been left for dead
I wouldn't believe them, feeling it must be true.

Next week the bloody Roll of Honour said
"Wounded and missing"—(That's the thing to do
When lads are left in shell-holes dying slow,
With nothing but blank sky and wounds that ache,
Moaning for water till they know
It's night, and then it's not worth while to wake!)

Good-bye, old lad! Remember me to God,
And tell Him that our politicians swear
They won't give in till Prussian Rule's been trod
Under the Heel of England ... Are you there? ...
Yes ... and the war won't end for at least two years;
But we've got stacks of men ... I'm blind with tears,
Staring into the dark. Cheero!
I wish they'd killed you in a decent show.

Photographs

(To Two Scots Lads)

Lying in dug-outs, joking idly, wearily;
Watching the candle guttering in the draught;
Hearing the great shells go high over us, eerily
Singing; how often have I turned over, and laughed

With pity and pride, photographs of all colours,
All sizes, subjects: khaki brothers in France;
Or mother's faces worn with countless dolours;
Or girls whose eyes were challenging and must dance,

Though in a picture only, a common cheap
Ill-taken card; and children—frozen, some
(Babies) waiting on Dicky-bird to peep
Out of the handkerchief that is his home

(But he's so shy!). And some with bright looks, calling
Delight across the miles of land and sea,
That not the dread of barrage suddenly falling
Could quite blot out—not mud nor lethargy.

Smiles and triumphant careless laughter. O
The pain of them, wide Earth's most sacred things!
Lying in dug-outs, hearing the great shells slow
Sailing mile-high, the heart mounts higher and sings.

But once—O why did he keep that bitter token
Of a dead Love?—that boy, who, suddenly moved,
Showed me, his eyes wet, his low talk broken,

A girl who better had not been beloved.

Breakfast

We ate our breakfast lying on our backs,
Because the shells were screeching overhead.
I bet a rasher to a loaf of bread
That Hull United would beat Halifax
When Jimmy Stainthorpe played full-back instead
of Billy Bradford. Ginger raised his head
And cursed, and took the bet; and dropt back dead.
We ate our breakfast lying on our backs,
Because the shells were screeching overhead.

Strange Meeting

It seemed that out of battle I escaped
Down some profound dull tunnel, long since scooped
Through granites which titanic wars had groined.

Yet also there encumbered sleepers groaned,
Too fast in thought or death to be bestirred.
Then, as I probed them, one sprang up, and stared
With piteous recognition in fixed eyes,
Lifting distressful hands, as if to bless.
And by his smile, I knew that sullen hall,—
By his dead smile I knew we stood in Hell.

With a thousand fears that vision's face was grained;
Yet no blood reached there from the upper ground,
And no guns thumped, or down the flues made moan.
"Strange friend," I said, "here is no cause to mourn."
"None," said that other, "save the undone years,
The hopelessness. Whatever hope is yours,
Was my life also; I went hunting wild
After the wildest beauty in the world,
Which lies not calm in eyes, or braided hair,
But mocks the steady running of the hour,
And if it grieves, grieves richlier than here.
For by my glee might many men have laughed,
And of my weeping something had been left,
Which must die now. I mean the truth untold,
The pity of war, the pity war distilled.
Now men will go content with what we spoiled.
Or, discontent, boil bloody, and be spilled.

They will be swift with swiftness of the tigress.
None will break ranks, though nations trek from progress.
Courage was mine, and I had mystery;
Wisdom was mine, and I had mastery:
To miss the march of this retreating world
Into vain citadels that are not walled.
Then, when much blood had clogged their chariot-wheels,
I would go up and wash them from sweet wells,
Even with truths that lie too deep for taint.
I would have poured my spirit without stint
But not through wounds; not on the cess of war.
Foreheads of men have bled where no wounds were.

"I am the enemy you killed, my friend.
I knew you in this dark: for so you frowned
Yesterday through me as you jabbed and killed.
I parried; but my hands were loath and cold.
Let us sleep now. . . ."

Futility

Move him into the sun—
Gently its touch awoke him once,
At home, whispering of fields half-sown.
Always it woke him, even in France,
Until this morning and this snow.
If anything might rouse him now
The kind old sun will know.

Think how it wakes the seeds—
Woke once the clays of a cold star.
Are limbs, so dear-achieved, are sides
Full-nerved, still warm, too hard to stir?
Was it for this the clay grew tall?
—O what made fatuous sunbeams toil
To break earth's sleep at all?

Attack

At dawn the ridge emerges massed and dun
In the wild purple of the glow'ring sun,
Smouldering through spouts of drifting smoke that shroud
The menacing scarred slope; and, one by one,
Tanks creep and topple forward to the wire.
The barrage roars and lifts. Then, clumsily bowed
With bombs and guns and shovels and battle-gear,
Men jostle and climb to, meet the bristling fire.
Lines of grey, muttering faces, masked with fear,
They leave their trenches, going over the top,
While time ticks blank and busy on their wrists,
And hope, with furtive eyes and grappling fists,
Flounders in mud. O Jesus, make it stop!

Repression of War Experience

Now light the candles; one; two; there's a moth;
What silly beggars they are to blunder in
And scorch their wings with glory, liquid flame—
No, no, not that,—it's bad to think of war,
When thoughts you've gagged all day come back to scare you;
And it's been proved that soldiers don't go mad
Unless they lose control of ugly thoughts
That drive them out to jabber among the trees.

Now light your pipe; look, what a steady hand.
Draw a deep breath; stop thinking; count fifteen,
And you're as right as rain ...
Why won't it rain? ...
I wish there'd be a thunder-storm to-night,
With bucketsful of water to sluice the dark,
And make the roses hang their dripping heads.

Books; what a jolly company they are,
Standing so quiet and patient on their shelves,
Dressed in dim brown, and black, and white, and green,
And every kind of colour. Which will you read?
Come on; O do read something; they're so wise.
I tell you all the wisdom of the world
Is waiting for you on those shelves; and yet
You sit and gnaw your nails, and let your pipe out,
And listen to the silence: on the ceiling
There's one big, dizzy moth that bumps and flutters;
And in the breathless air outside the house
The garden waits for something that delays.

There must be crowds of ghosts among the trees,—
Not people killed in battle,—they're in France,—
But horrible shapes in shrouds--old men who died
Slow, natural deaths,—old men with ugly souls,
Who wore their bodies out with nasty sins.

* * *

You're quiet and peaceful, summering safe at home;
You'd never think there was a bloody war on! ...
O yes, you would ... why, you can hear the guns.
Hark! Thud, thud, thud,—quite soft ... they never cease—
Those whispering guns—O Christ, I want to go out
And screech at them to stop—I'm going crazy;
I'm going stark, staring mad because of the guns.

Grass

Pile the bodies high at Austerlitz and Waterloo.
Shovel them under and let me work—
I am the grass; I cover all.

And pile them high at Gettysburg
And pile them high at Ypres and Verdun.
Shovel them under and let me work.
Two years, ten years, and passengers ask the conductor:
What place is this?
Where are we now?

I am the grass.
Let me work.

Dawn on the Somme

Last night rain fell over the scarred plateau
And now from the dark horizon, dazzling, flies
Arrow on fire-plumed arrow to the skies
Shot from the bright arc of Apollo's bow;
And from the wild and writhen waste below,
From flashing pools and mounds lit one by one,
O is it mist or are these companies
Of morning heroes who arise, arise
With thrusting arms, with limbs and hair aglow
Toward the risen god, upon whose brow
Burns the gold laurel of all victories,
Hero and hero's god, th' invincible Sun?

God! How I hate you, you young cheerful men"

God! How I hate you, you young cheerful men,
Whose pious poetry blossoms on your graves

As soon as you are in them, nurtured up
By the salt of your corruption, and the tears
Of mothers, local vicars, college deans,
And flanked by prefaces and photographs
From all you minor poet friends—the fools—
Who paint their sentimental elegies
Where sure, no angel treads; and, living, share
The dead's brief immortality
Oh Christ!
To think that one could spread the ductile wax
Of his fluid youth to Oxford's glowing fires
And take her seal so ill! Hark how one chants—
"Oh happy to have lived these epic days"—
"These epic days"! And he'd been to France,
And seen the trenches, glimpsed the huddled dead
In the periscope, hung in the rusting wire:
Chobed by their sickley fœtor, day and night
Blown down his throat: stumbled through ruined hearths,
Proved all that muddy brown monotony,
Where blood's the only coloured thing. Perhaps
Had seen a man killed, a sentry shot at night,
Hunched as he fell, his feet on the firing-step,
His neck against the back slope of the trench,
And the rest doubled up between, his head
Smashed like and egg-shell, and the warm grey brain

Spattered all bloody on the parados:
Had flashed a torch on his face, and known his friend,
Shot, breathing hardly, in ten minutes—gone!
Yet still God's in His heaven, all is right
In the best possible of worlds. The woe,
Even His scaled eyes must see, is partial, only
A seeming woe, we cannot understand.
God loves us, God looks down on this out strife
And smiles in pity, blows a pipe at times
And calls some warriors home. We do not die,
God would not let us, He is too "intense,"
Too "passionate," a whole day sorrows He
Because a grass-blade dies. How rare life is!
On earth, the love and fellowship of men,
Men sternly banded: banded for what end?
Banded to maim and kill their fellow men—
For even Huns are men. In heaven above
A genial umpire, a good judge of sport,
Won't let us hurt each other! Let's rejoice
God keeps us faithful, pens us still in fold.
Ah, what a faith is ours (almost, it seems,
Large as a mustard-seed)—we trust and trust,
Nothing can shake us! Ah, how good God is
To suffer us to be born just now, when youth
That else would rust, can slake his blade in gore,
Where very God Himself does seem to walk
The bloody fields of Flanders He so loves!

Spring Offensive

Halted against the shade of a last hill,
They fed, and, lying easy, were at ease
And, finding comfortable chests and knees
Carelessly slept.
But many there stood still
To face the stark, blank sky beyond the ridge,
Knowing their feet had come to the end of the world.
Marvelling they stood, and watched the long grass swirled
By the May breeze, murmurous with wasp and midge,
For though the summer oozed into their veins
Like the injected drug for their bones' pains,
Sharp on their souls hung the imminent line of grass,
Fearfully flashed the sky's mysterious glass.

Hour after hour they ponder the warm field—
And the far valley behind, where the buttercups
Had blessed with gold their slow boots coming up,
Where even the little brambles would not yield,
But clutched and clung to them like sorrowing hands;
They breathe like trees unstirred.
Till like a cold gust thrilled the little word
At which each body and its soul begird
And tighten them for battle. No alarms
Of bugles, no high flags, no clamorous haste—
Only a lift and flare of eyes that faced
The sun, like a friend with whom their love is done.
O larger shone that smile against the sun,—
Mightier than his whose bounty these have spurned.

So, soon they topped the hill, and raced together

Over an open stretch of herb and heather
Exposed. And instantly the whole sky burned
With fury against them; and soft sudden cups
Opened in thousands for their blood; and the green slopes
Chasmed and steepened sheer to infinite space.

Of them who running on that last high place
Leapt to swift unseen bullets, or went up
On the hot blast and fury of hell's upsurge,
Or plunged and fell away past this world's verge,
Some say God caught them even before they fell.
But what say such as from existence' brink
Ventured but drave too swift to sink.
The few who rushed in the body to enter hell,
And there out-fiending all its fiends and flames
With superhuman inhumanities,
Long-famous glories, immemorial shames—
And crawling slowly back, have by degrees
Regained cool peaceful air in wonder—
Why speak they not of comrades that went under?

Epitaph On My Days in Hospital

I found in you a holy place apart,
Sublime endurance, God in man revealed,
Where mending broken bodies slowly healed
My broken heart

War Mothers

There is something in the sound of drum and fife
That stirs all the savage instincts into life.

In the old times of peace we went our ways,
Through proper days
Of little joys and tasks. Lonely at times,
When from the steeple sounded wedding chimes,
Telling to all the world some maid was wife—
But taking patiently our part in life
As it was portioned us by Church and State,
Believing it our fate.
Our thoughts all chaste
Held yet a secret wish to love and mate
Ere youth and virtue should go quite to waste.
But men we criticised for lack of strength,
And kept them at arm's length.
Then the war came—
The world was all aflame!
The men we had thought dull and void of power
Were heroes in an hour.
He who had seemed a slave to petty greed
Showed masterful in that great time of need.
He who had plotted for his neighbour's pelf,
Now for his fellows offers up himself.
And we were only women, forced by war
To sacrifice the things worth living for.

Something within us broke,
Something within us woke,

The wild cave-woman spoke.

When we heard the sound of drumming,
As our soldiers went to camp,
Heard them tramp, tramp, tramp;
As we watched to see them coming,
And they looked at us and smiled
(Yes, looked back at us and smiled),
As they filed along by hillock and by hollow,
Then our hearts were so beguiled
That, for many and many a day,
We dreamed we heard them say,
'Oh, follow, follow, follow!'
And the distant, rolling drum
Called us 'Come, come, come!'
Till our virtue seemed a thing to give away.

War had swept ten thousand years away from earth.
We were primal once again.
There were males, not modern men;
We were females meant to bring their sons to birth.
And we could not wait for any formal rite,
We could hear them calling to us, 'Come to-night;
For to-morrow, at the dawn,
We move on!'
And the drum
Bellowed, 'Come, come, come!'
And the fife
Whistled, 'Life, life, life!'

So they moved on and fought and bled and died;
Honoured and mourned, they are the nation's pride.
We fought our battles, too, but with the tide
Of our red blood, we gave the world new lives.

Because we were not wives
We are dishonoured. Is it noble, then,
To break God's laws only by killing men
To save one's country from destruction?
We took no man's life but gave our chastity,
And sinned the ancient sin
To plant young trees and fill felled forests in.

Oh, clergy of the land,
Bible in hand,
All reverently you stand,
On holy thoughts intent
While barren wives receive the sacrament!
Had you the open visions you could see
Phantoms of infants murdered in the womb,
Who never knew a cradle or a tomb,
Hovering about these wives accusingly.

Bestow the sacrament! Their sins are not well known—
Ours to the four winds of the earth are blown.

Glory of Women

You love us when we're heroes, home on leave,
Or wounded in a mentionable place.
You worship decorations; you believe
That chivalry redeems the war's disgrace.
You make us shells. You listen with delight,
By tales of dirt and danger fondly thrilled.
You crown our distant ardours while we fight,
And mourn our laurelled memories when we're killed.
You can't believe that British troops "retire"
When hell's last horror breaks them, and they run,
Trampling the terrible corpses—blind with blood.
O German mother dreaming by the fire,
While you are knitting socks to send your son
His face is trodden deeper in the mud.

Smile, Smile, Smile

Head to limp head, the sunk-eyed wounded scanned
Yesterday's Mail; the casualties (typed small)
And (large) Vast Booty from our Latest Haul.
Also, they read of Cheap Homes, not yet planned;
"For," said the paper, "when this war is done
The men's first instinct will be making homes.
Meanwhile their foremost need is aerodromes,
It being certain war has just begun.
Peace would do wrong to our undying dead,—
The sons we offered might regret they died
If we got nothing lasting in their stead.
We must be solidly indemnified.
Though all be worthy Victory which all bought.
We rulers sitting in this ancient spot
Would wrong our very selves if we forgot
The greatest glory will be theirs who fought,
Who kept this nation in integrity."
Nation?—The half-limbed readers did not chafe
But smiled at one another curiously
Like secret men who know their secret safe.
(This is the thing they know and never speak,
That England one by one had fled to France
Not many elsewhere now save under France).
Pictures of these broad smiles appear each week,
And people in whose voice real feeling rings
Say: How they smile! They're happy now, poor things.

S. I. W.

I will to the King,
And offer him consolation in his trouble,
For that man there has set his teeth to die,
And being one that hates obedience,
Discipline, and orderliness of life,
I cannot mourn him.

1. THE PROLOGUE

Patting good-bye, doubtless they told the lad
He'd always show the Hun a brave man's face;
Father would sooner him dead than in disgrace,—
Was proud to see him going, aye, and glad.
Perhaps his mother whimpered how she'd fret
Until he got a nice safe wound to nurse.
Sisters would wish girls too could shoot, charge, curse …
Brothers—would send his favourite cigarette.
Each week, month after month, they wrote the same,
Thinking him sheltered in some Y.M. Hut,
Because he said so, writing on his butt
Where once an hour a bullet missed its aim
And misses teased the hunger of his brain.
His eyes grew old with wincing, and his hand
Reckless with ague. Courage leaked, as sand
From the best sand-bags after years of rain.
But never leave, wound, fever, trench-foot, shock,
Untrapped the wretch. And death seemed still withheld
For torture of lying machinally shelled,
At the pleasure of this world's Powers who'd run amok.

He'd seen men shoot their hands, on night patrol.
Their people never knew. Yet they were vile.
'Death sooner than dishonour, that's the style!'
So Father said.

II. THE ACTION

One dawn, our wire patrol
Carried him. This time, Death had not missed.
We could do nothing but wipe his bleeding cough.
Could it be accident? - Rifles go off…
Not sniped? No. (Later they found the English ball.)

III. THE POEM

It was the reasoned crisis of his soul
Against more days of inescapable thrall,
Against infrangibly wired and blind trench wall
Curtained with fire, roofed in with creeping fire,
Slow grazing fire, that would not burn him whole
But kept him for death's promises and scoff,
And life's half-promising, and both their riling.

IV. THE EPILOGUE

With him they buried the muzzle his teeth had kissed,
And truthfully wrote the Mother, 'Tim died smiling'.

And There Was a Great Calm

(On the Signing of the Armistice, 11 Nov. 1918)

I

There had been years of Passion—scorching, cold,
And much Despair, and Anger heaving high,
Care whitely watching, Sorrows manifold,
Among the young, among the weak and old,
And the pensive Spirit of Pity whispered, "Why?"

II

Men had not paused to answer. Foes distraught
Pierced the thinned peoples in a brute-like blindness,
Philosophies that sages long had taught,
And Selflessness, were as an unknown thought,
And "Hell!" and "Shell!" were yapped at Lovingkindness.

III

The feeble folk at home had grown full-used
To 'dug-outs', 'snipers', 'Huns', from the war-adept
In the mornings heard, and at evetides perused;
To day-dreamt men in millions, when they mused—
To nightmare-men in millions when they slept.

IV

Waking to wish existence timeless, null,
Sirius they watched above where armies fell;
He seemed to check his flapping when, in the lull

Of night a boom came thencewise, like the dull
Plunge of a stone dropped into some deep well.

V

So, when old hopes that earth was bettering slowly
Were dead and damned, there sounded 'War is done!'
One morrow. Said the bereft, and meek, and lowly,
'Will men some day be given to grace? yea, wholly,
And in good sooth, as our dreams used to run?'

VI

Breathless they paused. Out there men raised their glance
To where had stood those poplars lank and lopped,
As they had raised it through the four years' dance
Of Death in the now familiar flats of France;
And murmured, 'Strange, this! How? All firing stopped?'

VII

Aye; all was hushed. The about-to-fire fired not,
The aimed-at moved away in trance-lipped song.
One checkless regiment slung a clinching shot
And turned. The Spirit of Irony smirked out, 'What?
Spoil peradventures woven of Rage and Wrong?'

VIII

Thenceforth no flying fires inflamed the gray,
No hurtlings shook the dewdrop from the thorn,
No moan perplexed the mute bird on the spray;
Worn horses mused: 'We are not whipped to-day;'
No weft-winged engines blurred the moon's thin horn.

IX

Calm fell. From Heaven distilled a clemency;
There was peace on earth, and silence in the sky;

Some could, some could not, shake off misery:
The Sinister Spirit sneered: 'It had to be!'
And again the Spirit of Pity whispered, 'Why?'

January 1919

What if I know, Liebknecht, who shot you dead.
Tiergarten trees unroll
staggering shadow, in spite of it all.
I am among the leaves; the inevitable
voices
have nothing left to say, the holed head
bleeding across a heap of progressive magazines;
torn from your face,
trees that turned around,
we do not sanctify the land with our wandering.
Look upon our children, they are mutilated.

Everyone Sang

Everyone suddenly burst out singing;
And I was filled with such delight
As prisoned birds must find in freedom,
Winging wildly across the white
Orchards and dark-green fields; on - on - and out of sight.

Everyone's voice was suddenly lifted;
And beauty came like the setting sun:
My heart was shaken with tears; and horror
Drifted away ... O, but Everyone
Was a bird; and the song was wordless; the singing will never be done.

The Cenotaph

Not yet will those measureless fields be green again
Where only yesterday the wild sweet blood of wonderful youth was shed;
There is a grave whose earth must hold too long, too deep a stain,
Though for ever over it we may speak as proudly as we may tread.
But here, where the watchers by lonely hearths from the thrust of an inward sword have more slowly bled,
We shall build the Cenotaph: Victory, winged, with Peace, winged too, at the column's head.
And over the stairway, at the foot—oh! here, leave desolate, passionate hands to spread
Violets, roses, and laurel with the small sweet twinkling country things
Speaking so wistfully of other Springs
From the little gardens of little places where son or sweetheart was born and bred.
In splendid sleep, with a thousand brothers
To lovers—to mothers
Here, too, lies he:
Under the purple, the green, the red,
It is all young life: it must break some women's hearts to see
Such a brave, gay coverlet to such a bed!
Only, when all is done and said,
God is not mocked and neither are the dead.
For this will stand in our Market-place—
Who'll sell, who'll buy
(Will you or I

Lie each to each with the better grace)?
While looking into every busy whore's and huckster's face
As they drive their bargains, is the Face
Of God: and some young, piteous, murdered face.

First Time In ["After the dread tales ... "]

After the dread tales and red yarns of the Line
Anything might have come to us; but the divine

Afterglow brought us up to a Welsh colony
Hiding in sandbag ditches, whispering consolatory

Soft foreign things. Then we were taken in
To low huts candle-lit, shaded close by slitten

Oilsheets, and there but boys gave us kind welcome,
So that we looked out as from the edge of home,
Sang us Welsh things, and changed all former notions
To human hopeful things. And the next day's guns
Nor any Line-pangs ever quite could blot out
That strangely beautiful entry to war's rout;
Candles they gave us, precious and shared over-rations—
Ulysses found little more in his wanderings without doubt.
'David of the White Rock', the 'Slumber Song'
so soft, and that
Beautiful tune to which roguish words by Welsh pit boys
Are sung—but never more beautiful
than here under the guns' noise.

Epitaphs of the War

1914-18

“EQUALITY OF SACRIFICE”

A. “I was a Have.” B. “I was a ‘have-not.’”
(Together). “What hast thou given which I gave not?”

A SERVANT

We were together since the War began.
He was my servant—and the better man.

A SON

My son was killed while laughing at some jest.
I would I knew
What it was, and it might serve me in a time when jests are few.

AN ONLY SON

I have slain none except my Mother. She
(Blessing her slayer) died of grief for me.

EX-CLERK

Pity not! The Army gave
Freedom to a timid slave:
In which Freedom did he find
Strength of body, will, and mind:
By which strength he came to prove
Mirth, Companionship, and Love:
For which Love to Death he went:
In which Death he lies content.

THE WONDER

Body and Spirit I surrendered whole
To harsh Instructors—and received a soul . . .
If mortal man could change me through and through
From all I was—what may The God not do?

HINDU SEPOY IN FRANCE

This man in his own country prayed we know not to what Powers.
We pray Them to reward him for his bravery in ours.

THE COWARD

I could not look on Death, which being known,
Men led me to him, blindfold and alone.

SHOCK

My name, my speech, my self I had forgot.
My wife and children came—I knew them not.
I died. My Mother followed. At her call
And on her bosom I remembered all.

A GRAVE NEAR CAIRO

Gods of the Nile, should this stout fellow here
Get out—get out! He knows not shame nor fear.

PELICANS IN THE WILDERNESS

A Grave near Halfa

The blown sand heaps on me, that none may learn
Where I am laid for whom my children grieve . . .
O wings that beat at dawning, ye return
Out of the desert to your young at eve!

TWO CANADIAN MEMORIALS

I

We giving all gained all.
Neither lament us nor praise.
Only in all things recall,
It is Fear, not Death that slays.

II

From little towns in a far land we came,
To save our honour and a world aflame.
By little towns in a far land we sleep;
And trust that world we won for you to keep!

THE FAVOUR

Death favoured me from the first, well knowing
I could not endure
To wait on him day by day. He quitted my betters and came
Whistling over the fields, and, when he had made all sure,
"Thy line is at end," he said, "but at least I have saved its name."

THE BEGINNER

On the first hour of my first day
In the front trench I fell.
(Children in boxes at a play
Stand up to watch it well.)

R.A.F. (AGED EIGHTEEN)

Laughing through clouds, his milk-teeth still unshed,
Cities and men he smote from overhead.
His deaths delivered, he returned to play
Childlike, with childish things now put away.

THE REFINED MAN

I was of delicate mind. I stepped aside for my needs,
Disdaining the common office.
I was seen from afar and killed . . .
How is this matter for mirth?
Let each man be judged by his deeds.
I have paid my price to live with myself on the terms that I willed.

NATIVE WATER-CARRIER (M.E.F.)

Prometheus brought down fire to men,
This brought up water.
The Gods are jealous—now, as then,
Giving no quarter.

BOMBED IN LONDON

On land and sea I strove with anxious care
To escape conscription. It was in the air!

THE SLEEPY SENTINAL

Faithless the watch that I kept: now I have none to keep.
I was slain because I slept: now I am slain I sleep.
Let no man reproach me again, whatever watch is unkept—
I sleep because I am slain. They slew me because I slept.

BATTERIES OUT OF AMMUNITION

If any mourn us in the workshop, say
We died because the shift kept holiday.

COMMON FORM

If any question why we died,
Tell them, because our fathers lied.

A DEAD STATESMAN

I could not dig: I dared not rob:
Therefore I lied to please the mob.
Now all my lies are proved untrue
And I must face the men I slew.
What tale shall serve me here among
Mine angry and defrauded young?

THE REBEL

If I had clamoured at Thy Gate
For gift of Life on Earth,
And, thrusting through the souls that wait,
Flung headlong into birth—
Even then, even then, for gin and snare
About my pathway spread,
Lord, I had mocked Thy thoughtful care
Before I joined the Dead!
But now? . . . I was beneath Thy Hand
Ere yet the Planets came.
And now—though Planets pass, I stand
The witness to Thy shame!

THE OBEDIENT

Daily, though no ears attended,
Did my prayers arise.
Daily, though no fire descended,
Did I sacrifice.
Though my darkness did not lift,
Though I faced no lighter odds,
Though the Gods bestowed no gift,
None the less,
None the less, I served the Gods!

A DRIFTER OFF TARENTUM

He from the wind-bitten
North with ship and companions descended,
Searching for eggs of death spawned by invisible hulls.
Many he found and drew forth.
Of a sudden the fishery ended
In flame and a clamours breath known to
the eye-pecking gulls.

DESTROYER IN COLLISION

For Fog and Fate no charm is found
To lighten or amend.
I, hurrying to my bride, was drowned—
Cut down by my best friend.

CONVOY ESCORT

I was a shepherd to fools
Causelessly bold or afraid.
They would not abide by my rules.
Yet they escaped. For I stayed.

UNKNOWN FEMALE CORPSE

Headless, lacking foot and hand,
Horrible I come to land.
I beseech all women's sons
Know I was a mother once.

RAPED AND REVENGED

One used and butchered me: another spied
Me broken—for which thing an hundred died.
So it was learned among the heathen hosts
How much a freeborn woman's favour costs.

SALONIKAN GRAVE

I have watched a thousand days
Push out and crawl into night
Slowly as tortoises.
Now I, too, follow these.
It is fever, and not the fight—
Time, not battle,—that slays.

THE BRIDEGROOM

Call me not false, beloved,
If, from thy scarce-known breast
So little time removed,
In other arms I rest.

For this more ancient bride,
Whom coldly I embrace,
Was constant at my side
Before I saw thy face.

Our marriage, often set—
By miracle delayed—
At last is consummate,
And cannot be unmade.

Live, then, whom Life shall cure,
Almost, of Memory,
And leave us to endure
Its immortality.

V.A.D. (MEDITERRANEAN)

Ah, would swift ships had never been,
for then we ne'er had found,
These harsh Aegean rocks between,
this little virgin drowned,
Whom neither spouse nor child shall mourn,
but men she nursed through pain
And—certain keels for whose return the heathen look in vain.

ACTORS

On a Memorial Tablet in Holy Trinity Church,
Stratford-on-Avon

We counterfeited once for your disport
Men's joy and sorrow: but our day has passed.
We pray you pardon all where we fell short—
Seeing we were your servants to this last.

JOURNALISTS

On a Panel in the Hall of the Institute of Journalists

We have served our day.
Hugh Selwyn Mauberley [Part I]
BY EZRA POUND
(Life and Contacts)

"Vocat aestus in umbram"
Nemesianus Ec. IV.
E. P. ODE POUR L'ÉLECTION DE SON SÉPULCHRE

For three years, out of key with his time,
He strove to resuscitate the dead art
Of poetry; to maintain "the sublime"
In the old sense. Wrong from the start—

No, hardly, but, seeing he had been born
In a half savage country, out of date;
Bent resolutely on wringing lilies from the acorn;
Capaneus; trout for factitious bait:

"Idmen gar toi panth, os eni Troie
Caught in the unstopped ear;
Giving the rocks small lee-way
The chopped seas held him, therefore, that year.

His true Penelope was Flaubert,
He fished by obstinate isles;

Observed the elegance of Circe's hair
Rather than the mottoes on sun-dials.

Unaffected by "the march of events,"
He passed from men's memory in l'an trentiesme
De son eage; the case presents
No adjunct to the Muses' diadem.

II

The age demanded an image
Of its accelerated grimace,
Something for the modern stage,
Not, at any rate, an Attic grace;

Not, not certainly, the obscure reveries
Of the inward gaze;
Better mendacities
Than the classics in paraphrase!

The "age demanded" chiefly a mould in plaster,
Made with no loss of time,
A prose kinema, not, not assuredly, alabaster
Or the "sculpture" of rhyme.

III

The tea-rose, tea-gown, etc.
Supplants the mousseline of Cos,
The pianola "replaces"
Sappho's barbitos.

Christ follows Dionysus,
Phallic and ambrosial
Made way for macerations;
Caliban casts out Ariel.

All things are a flowing,
Sage Heracleitus says;
But a tawdry cheapness
Shall reign throughout our days.

Even the Christian beauty
Defects—after Samothrace;
We see to kalon
Decreed in the market place.

Faun's flesh is not to us,
Nor the saint's vision.
We have the press for wafer;
Franchise for circumcision.

All men, in law, are equals.
Free of Peisistratus,
We choose a knave or an eunuch
To rule over us.

A bright Apollo,

tin andra, tin eroa, tina theon,
What god, man, or hero
Shall I place a tin wreath upon?

IV

These fought, in any case,
and some believing, pro domo, in any case ...

Some quick to arm,
some for adventure,
some from fear of weakness,
some from fear of censure,

some for love of slaughter, in imagination,
learning later ...
some in fear, learning love of slaughter;
Died some pro patria, non dulce non et decor" ...
walked eye-deep in hell
believing in old men's lies, then unbelieving
came home, home to a lie, home to many deceits,
home to old lies and new infamy;
usury age-old and age-thick
and liars in public places.

Daring as never before, wastage as never before.
Young blood and high blood,
Fair cheeks, and fine bodies;
fortitude as never before
frankness as never before,
disillusions as never told in the old days,
hysterias, trench confessions,
laughter out of dead bellies.

V

There died a myriad,
And of the best, among them,
For an old bitch gone in the teeth,
For a botched civilization.

Charm, smiling at the good mouth,
Quick eyes gone under earth's lid,

For two gross of broken statues,
For a few thousand battered books.

YEUX GLAUQUES

Gladstone was still respected,
When John Ruskin produced
"Kings Treasuries"; Swinburne
And Rossetti still abused.

Foetid Buchanan lifted up his voice
When that faun's head of hers
Became a pastime for
Painters and adulterers.

The Burne-Jones cartons
Have preserved her eyes;
Still, at the Tate, they teach
Cophetua to rhapsodize;

Thin like brook-water,
With a vacant gaze.
The English Rubaiyat was still-born
In those days.

The thin, clear gaze, the same
Still darts out faun-like from the half-ruin'd face,
Questing and passive ....
"Ah, poor Jenny's case" ...

Bewildered that a world
Shows no surprise
At her last maquero's
Adulteries.

"SIENA MI FE', DISFECEMI MAREMMA'"

Among the pickled foetuses and bottled bones,
Engaged in perfecting the catalogue,
I found the last scion of the
Senatorial families of Strasbourg, Monsieur Verog.

For two hours he talked of Gallifet;
Of Dowson; of the Rhymers' Club;
Told me how Johnson (Lionel) died
By falling from a high stool in a pub ...

But showed no trace of alcohol
At the autopsy, privately performed—
Tissue preserved—the pure mind
Arose toward Newman as the whiskey warmed.

Dowson found harlots cheaper than hotels;
Headlam for uplift; Image impartially imbued
With raptures for Bacchus, Terpsichore and the Church.
So spoke the author of "The Dorian Mood,"

M. Verog, out of step with the decade,
Detached from his contemporaries,
Neglected by the young,
Because of these reveries.

BRENNEBAUM

The sky-like limpid eyes,
The circular infant's face,
The stiffness from spats to collar
Never relaxing into grace;

The heavy memories of Horeb, Sinai and the forty years,
Showed only when the daylight fell
Level across the face
Of Brennbaum "The Impeccable."

MR. NIXON

In the cream gilded cabin of his steam yacht
Mr. Nixon advised me kindly, to advance with fewer
Dangers of delay. "Consider
"Carefully the reviewer.

"I was as poor as you are;
"When I began I got, of course,
"Advance on royalties, fifty at first," said Mr. Nixon,
"Follow me, and take a column,
"Even if you have to work free.

"Butter reviewers. From fifty to three hundred
"I rose in eighteen months;
"The hardest nut I had to crack
"Was Dr. Dundas.

"I never mentioned a man but with the view
"Of selling my own works.
"The tip's a good one, as for literature
"It gives no man a sinecure."

And no one knows, at sight a masterpiece.
And give up verse, my boy,
There's nothing in it."

* * * *

Likewise a friend of Bloughram's once advised me:
Don't kick against the pricks,
Accept opinion. The "Nineties" tried your game

And died, there's nothing in it.

X

Beneath the sagging roof
The stylist has taken shelter,
Unpaid, uncelebrated,
At last from the world's welter

Nature receives him,
With a placid and uneducated mistress
He exercises his talents
And the soil meets his distress.

The haven from sophistications and contentions
Leaks through its thatch;
He offers succulent cooking;
The door has a creaking latch.

XI

"Conservatrix of Milésien"
Habits of mind and feeling,
Possibly. But in Ealing
With the most bank-clerkly of Englishmen?

No, "Milésian" is an exaggeration.
No instinct has survived in her
Older than those her grandmother
Told her would fit her station.

XII

"Daphne with her thighs in bark
Stretches toward me her leafy hands,"—
Subjectively. In the stuffed-satin drawing-room
I await The Lady Valentine's commands,

Knowing my coat has never been
Of precisely the fashion
To stimulate, in her,
A durable passion;

Doubtful, somewhat, of the value
Of well-gowned approbation
Of literary effort,
But never of The Lady Valentine's vocation:

Poetry, her border of ideas,
The edge, uncertain, but a means of blending
With other strata
Where the lower and higher have ending;

A hook to catch the Lady Jane's attention,
A modulation toward the theatre,
Also, in the case of revolution,
A possible friend and comforter.

* * * *

Conduct, on the other hand, the soul
"Which the highest cultures have nourished"
To Fleet St. where
Dr. Johnson flourished;

Beside this thoroughfare
The sale of half-hose has
Long since superseded the cultivation
Of Pierian roses.

Envoi (1919)

Go, dumb-born book,
Tell her that sang me once that song of Lawes:
Hadst thou but song
As thou hast subjects known,
Then were there cause in thee that should condone
Even my faults that heavy upon me lie
And build her glories their longevity.

Tell her that sheds
Such treasure in the air,
Recking naught else but that her graces give
Life to the moment,
I would bid them live
As roses might, in magic amber laid,
Red overwrought with orange and all made
One substance and one colour
Braving time.

Tell her that goes
With song upon her lips
But sings not out the song, nor knows
The maker of it, some other mouth,
May be as fair as hers,
Might, in new ages, gain her worshippers,
When our two dusts with Waller's shall be laid,
Siftings on siftings in oblivion,
Till change hath broken down
All things save Beauty alone.

A. E. F.

There will be a rusty gun on the wall, sweetheart,
The rifle grooves curling with flakes of rust.
A spider will make a silver string nest in the
darkest, warmest corner of it.
The trigger and the range-finder, they too will be rusty.
And no hands will polish the gun, and it will hang on the wall.
Forefingers and thumbs will point casually toward it.
It will be spoken among half-forgotten, whished-to-be-
forgotten things.
They will tell the spider: Go on, you're doing good work.

To E. T.

I slumbered with your poems on my breast
Spread open as I dropped them half-read through
Like dove wings on a figure on a tomb
To see, if in a dream they brought of you,

I might not have the chance I missed in life
Through some delay, and call you to your face
First soldier, and then poet, and then both,
Who died a soldier-poet of your race.

I meant, you meant, that nothing should remain
Unsaid between us, brother, and this remained—
And one thing more that was not then to say:
The Victory for what it lost and gained.

You went to meet the shell's embrace of fire
On Vimy Ridge; and when you fell that day
The war seemed over more for you than me,
But now for me than you—the other way.

How over, though, for even me who knew
The foe thrust back unsafe beyond the Rhine,
If I was not to speak of it to you
And see you pleased once more with words of mine?

In Memory of George Calderon

Wisdom and Valour, Faith,
Justice,—the lofty names
Of virtue's quest and prize,—
What is each but a cold wraith
Until it lives in a man
And looks thro' a man's eyes?

On Chivalry as I muse,
The spirit so high and clear
It cannot soil with aught
It meets of foul misuse;
It turns wherever burns
The flame of a brave thought;

And wheresoever the moan
Of the helpless and betrayed
Calls, from near or far,
It replies as to its own
Need, and is armed and goes
Straight to its sure pole—star;—

No legendary knight
Renowned in an ancient cause
I warm my thought upon.
There comes to the mind's sight
One whom I knew, whose hand
Grasped mine: George Calderon.

Him now as of old I see

Carrying his head with an air
Courteous and virile,
With the charm of a nature free,
Daring, resourceful, prompt,
In his frank and witty smile.

By Oxford towers and streams
Who shone among us all
In body and brain so bold?
Who shaped so firm his themes
Crystal—hard in debate?
And who hid a heart less cold?

Lover of strange tongues,
Whether in snowy Russia,
Or tropic island bowers
Listening to the songs
Of the soft—eyed islanders,
Crowned with Tahitian flowers,

A maker of friends he went.
Yet who divined him wholly
Or his secret chivalries?—
Was all that accomplishment,
Wit, alertness, grace,
But a kind of blithe disguise?

Restless in curious thought
And subtle exploring mind,
He mixt his modern vein
With a strain remotely brought
From an older blood than ours,
Proud loyalties of Spain.

Was it the soul of a sword?

For a bright sword leapt from sheath
Upon that August day
When war's full thunder stored
Over Europe, suddenly crashed,
And a choice upon each man lay.

Others had left their youth
In the taming years; and some
Doubted; some made moan.
To meet the peril of truth
With aught but a gay courage
Was not for Calderon.

Wounded from France he came.
His spirit halted not;
In that long battle afar,
Fruitless in all but fame,
Athos and Ida saw
Where sank his gallant star.

O well could I set my mood
To a mournful falling measure
For a friend dear and dead!
And well could memory brood
Singing of youth's delight
And lost adventure fled.

But that so fearless friend
With his victorious smile
My mourning mood has chid.
He went to the very end;
He counted not the cost;
What he believed, he did.

War and Peace

In sodden trenches I have heard men speak,
Though numb and wretched, wise and witty things;
And loved them for the stubbornness that clings
Longest to laughter when Death's pulleys creak;

And seeing cool nurses move on tireless feet
To do abominable things with grace,
Deemed them sweet sisters in that haunted place
Where, with child's voices, strong men howl or bleat.

Yet now those men lay stubborn courage by,
Riding dull-eyed and silent in the train
To old men's stools; or sell gay-coloured socks
And listen fearfully for Death; so I
Love the low-laughing girls, who now again
Go daintily, in thin and flowery frocks.

Trench Poets

I knew a man, he was my chum,
but he grew blacker every day,
and would not brush the flies away,
nor blanch however fierce the hum
of passing shells; I used to read,
to rouse him, random things from Donne—
like "Get with child a mandrake-root."
But you can tell he was far gone,
for he lay gaping, mackerel-eyed,
and stiff, and senseless as a post
even when that old poet cried
"I long to talk with some old lover's ghost."

I tried the Elegies one day,
But he, because he heard me say:
"What needst thou have no more covering than a man?"
grinned nastily, and so I knew
the worms had got his brains at last.
There was one thing that I might do
to starve the worms; I racked my head
for healthy things and quoted Maud.
His grin got worse and I could see
he sneered at passion's purity.
He stank so badly, though we were great chums
I had to leave him; then rats ate his thumbs.

For a War Memorial

(SUGGESTED INSCRIPTION PROBABLY NOT SUGGESTED BY THE COMMITTEE)

The hucksters haggle in the mart
The cars and carts go by;
Senates and schools go droning on;
For dead things cannot die.

A storm stooped on the place of tombs
With bolts to blast and rive;
But these be names of many men
The lightning found alive.

If usurers rule and rights decay
And visions view once more
Great Carthage like a golden shell
Gape hollow on the shore,

Still to the last of crumbling time
Upon this stone be read
How many men of England died
To prove they were not dead.

Festubert, 1916

Tired with dull grief, grown old before my day,
I sit in solitude and only hear
Long silent laughters, murmurings of dismay,
The lost intensities of hope and fear;
In those old marshes yet the rifles lie,
On the thin breastwork flutter the grey rags,
The very books I read are there—and I
Dead as the men I loved, wait while life drags

Its wounded length from those sad streets of war
Into green places here, that were my own;
But now what once was mine is mine no more,
I seek such neighbours here and I find none.
With such strong gentleness and tireless will
Those ruined houses seared themselves in me,
Passionate I look for their dumb story still,
And the charred stub outspeaks the living tree.

I rise up at the singing of a bird
And scarcely knowing slink along the lane,
I dare not give a soul a look or word
For all have homes and none's at home in vain:
Deep red the rose burned in the grim redoubt,
The self-sown wheat around was like a flood,
In the hot path the lizards lolled time out,
The saints in broken shrines were bright as blood.

Sweet Mary's shrine between the sycamores!
There we would go, my friend of friends and I,

And snatch long moments from the grudging wars;
Whose dark made light intense to see them by ...
Shrewd bit the morning fog, the whining shots
Spun from the wrangling wire; then in warm swoon
The sun hushed all but the cool orchard plots,
We crept in the tall grass and slept till noon.

Elegy in a Country Churchyard

The men that worked for England
They have their graves at home:
And birds and bees of England
About the cross can roam.

But they that fought for England,
Following a falling star,
Alas, alas for England
They have their graves afar.

And they that rule in England,
In stately conclave met,
Alas, alas for England
They have no graves as yet.

Epitaph on an Army of Mercenaries

These, in the days when heaven was falling,
The hour when earth's foundations fled,
Followed their mercenary calling
And took their wages and are dead.

Their shoulders held the sky suspended;
They stood, and the earth's foundations stay;
What God abandoned, these defended,
And saved the sum of things for pay.

"Soldier from the wars returning"

Soldier from the wars returning,
Spoiler of the taken town,
Here is ease that asks not earning;
Turn you in and sit you down.

Peace is come and wars are over,
Welcome you and welcome all,
While the charger crops the clover
And his bridle hangs in stall.

Now no more of winters biting,
Filth in trench from fall to spring,
Summers full of sweat and fighting
For the Kesar or the King.

Rest you, charger, rust you, bridle;
Kings and kesars, keep your pay;
Soldier, sit you down and idle
At the inn of night for aye.

I Saw England — July Night

She was a village

Of lovely knowledge
The high roads left her aside, she was forlorn, a maid —
Water ran there, dusk hid her, she climbed four-wayed.
Brown-gold windows showed last folk not yet asleep;
Water ran, was a centre of silence deep,
Fathomless deeps of pricked sky, almost fathomless
Hallowed an upward gaze in pale satin of blue.
And I was happy indeed, of mind, soul, body even
Having got given
A sign undoubtful of a dear England few
Doubt, not many have seen,
That Will Squele he knew and was so shriven.
Home of Twelfth Night — Edward Thomas by Arras fallen,
Borrow and Hardy, Sussex tales out of Roman heights callen.
No madrigals or field-songs to my all reverent whim;
Till I got back I was dumb.

Laventie

One would remember still
Meadows and low hill
Laventie was, as to the line and elm row
Growing through green strength wounded,
as home elms grow.
Shimmer of summer there and blue autumn mists
Seen from trench-ditch winding in mazy twists.
The Australian gunners in close flowery hiding
Cunning found out at last, and smashed in
the unspeakable lists.
And the guns in the smashed wood thumping and grinding.

The letters written there, and received there,
Books, cakes, cigarettes in a parish of famine,
And leaks in rainy times with general all-damning.
The crater, and carrying of gas cylinders on two sticks
(Pain past comparison and far past right agony gone)
Strained hopelessly of heart and frame at first fix.

Café-au-lait in dug-outs on Tommies' cookers,
Cursed minniewerfs, thirst in eighteen-hour summer.
The Australian miners clayed, and the being afraid
Before strafes, sultry August dusk time than Death dumber
—
And the cooler hush after the strafe, and the long night wait
—
The relief of first dawn, the crawling out to look at it,
Wonder divine of Dawn, man hesitating before Heaven's
gate.

(Though not on Coopers where music fire took at it,
Though not as at Framilode beauty where
body did shake at it)
Yet the dawn with aeroplanes crawling high at Heaven's gate
Lovely aerial beetles of wonderful scintillate
Strangest interest, and puffs of soft purest white —
Soaking light, dispersing colouring for fancy's delight.

Of Maconachie, Paxton, Tickler, and Gloucester's Stephens;
Fray Bentos, Spiller and Baker, odds and evens
Of trench food, but the everlasting clean craving
For bread, the pure thing, blessed beyond saving.
Canteen disappointments, and the keen boy braving
Bullets or such for grouse roused surprisingly through
(Halfway) Stand-to.
And the shell nearly blunted my razor at shaving;
Tilleloy, Pauquissart, Neuve Chapelle, and mud like glue.

But Laventie, most of all, I think is to soldiers
The Town itself with plane trees, and small-spa air;
And vin, rouge-blanc, chocolat, citron, grenadine:
One might buy in small delectable cafés there.
The broken church, and vegetable fields bare;
Neat French market town look so clean,
And the clarity, amiability of North French air.

Like water flowing beneath the dark plough and high Heaven,
Music's delight to please the poet pack-marching there.

The Anxious Dead

O guns, fall silent till the dead men hear Above their heads
the legions pressing on:
(These fought their fight in time of bitter fear,
And died not knowing how the day had gone.)

O flashing muzzles, pause, and let them see The coming
dawn that streaks the sky afar;
Then let your mighty chorus witness be
To them, and Caesar, that we still make war.

Tell them, O guns, that we have heard their call, That we have
sworn, and will not turn aside,
That we will onward till we win or fall,
That we will keep the faith for which they died.

Bid them be patient, and some day, anon,
They shall feel earth enwrapt in silence deep;
Shall greet, in wonderment, the quiet dawn,
And in content may turn them to their sleep.

The Warrior

He wrought in poverty, the dull grey days,
But with the night his little lamp-lit room
Was bright with battle flame, or through a haze Of smoke
that stung his eyes he heard the boom Of Bluecher's guns;
he shared Almeida's scars, And from the close-packed deck,
about to die, Looked up and saw the "Birkenhead"'s tall spars
Weave wavering lines across the Southern sky:

Or in the stifling 'tween decks, row on row,
At Aboukir, saw how the dead men lay;
Charged with the fiercest in Busaco's strife,
Brave dreams are his -- the flick'ring lamp burns low --
Yet couraged for the battles of the day

He goes to stand full face to face with life.

Isandlwana

Scarlet coats, and crash o' the band,
The grey of a pauper's gown,
A soldier's grave in Zululand, And a woman in Brecon Town.

My little lad for a soldier boy, (Mothers o' Brecon Town!)
My eyes for tears and his for joy When he went from Brecon
Town, His for the flags and the gallant sights
His for the medals and his for the fights, And mine for the
dreary, rainy nights
At home in Brecon Town.

They say he's laid beneath a tree,
(Come back to Brecon Town!)
Shouldn't I know? -- I was there to see:
(It's far to Brecon Town!)
It's me that keeps it trim and drest
With a briar there and a rose by his breast -- The English
flowers he likes the best
That I bring from Brecon Town.

And I sit beside him -- him and me,
(We're back to Brecon Town.)
To talk of the things that used to be
(Grey ghosts of Brecon Town);
I know the look o' the land and sky,
And the bird that builds in the tree near by, And times
I hear the jackals cry,
And me in Brecon Town.

Golden grey on miles of sand The dawn comes creeping
down; It's day in far off Zululand
And night in Brecon Town.

The Unconquered Dead

"... defeated, with great loss."
Not we the conquered!
Not to us the blame
Of them that flee, of them that basely yield;
Nor ours the shout of victory, the fame
Of them that vanquish in a stricken field.

That day of battle in the dusty heat
We lay and heard the bullets swish and sing
Like scythes amid the over-ripened wheat,
And we the harvest of their garnering.

Some yielded, No, not we!
Not we, we swear By these our wounds;
this trench upon the hill
Where all the shell-strewn earth is seamed and bare,
Was ours to keep; and lo! we have it still.

We might have yielded, even we, but death
Came for our helper; like a sudden flood
The crashing darkness fell; our painful breath
We drew with gasps amid the choking blood.

The roar fell faint and farther off, and soon Sank to a foolish
humming in our ears, Like crickets in the long, hot afternoon
Among the wheat fields of the olden years.

Before our eyes a boundless wall of red
Shot through by sudden streaks of jagged pain! Then a

slow-gathering darkness overhead
And rest came on us like a quiet rain.

Not we the conquered! Not to us the shame, Who hold our earthen ramparts, nor shall cease
To hold them ever; victors we, who came
In that fierce moment to our honoured peace.

The Captan 1797

Here all the day she swings from tide to tide, Here all night
long she tugs a rusted chain, A masterless hulk that was a ship
of pride, Yet unashamed: her memories remain.

It was Nelson in the `Captain', Cape St. Vincent far alee,
With the `Vanguard' leading s'uth'ard in the haze --
Little Jervis and the Spaniards and the fight that was to be,
Twenty-seven Spanish battleships, great bullies of the sea,
And the `Captain' there to find her day of days.

Right into them the `Vanguard' leads, but with a sudden tack
The Spaniards double swiftly on their trail;
Now Jervis overshoots his mark, like some too eager pack,
He will not overtake them, haste he e'er so greatly back, But
Nelson and the `Captain' will not fail.

Like a tigress on her quarry leaps the `Captain' from her
place, To lie across the fleeing squadron's way:
Heavy odds and heavy onslaught, gun to gun and face to face,
Win the ship a name of glory, win the men a death of grace,
For a little hold the Spanish fleet in play.

Ended now the "Captain"'s battle, stricken sore she falls aside
Holding still her foemen, beaten to the knee:
As the `Vanguard' drifted past her, "Well done, `Captain',"
Jervis cried, Rang the cheers of men that conquered, ran
the blood of men that died, And the ship had won her
immortality.

Lo! here her progeny of steel and steam,
A funnelled monster at her mooring swings: Still, in
our hearts, we see her pennant stream, And "Well done,
`Captain'," like a trumpet rings.

The Song of the Derelict

Ye have sung me your songs, ye have chanted your rimes
(I scorn your beguiling, O sea!)
Ye fondle me now, but to strike me betimes.
(A treacherous lover, the sea!)
Once I saw as I lay, half-awash in the night
A hull in the gloom -- a quick hail -- and a light
And I lurched o'er to leeward and saved her for spite From
the doom that ye meted to me.

I was sister to `Terrible', seventy-four,
(Yo ho! for the swing of the sea!)
And ye sank her in fathoms a thousand or more
(Alas! for the might of the sea!)
Ye taunt me and sing me her fate for a sign!
What harm can ye wreak more on me or on mine? Ho
braggart! I care not for boasting of thine --
A fig for the wrath of the sea!

Some night to the lee of the land I shall steal,
(Heigh-ho to be home from the sea!)
No pilot but Death at the rudderless wheel,
(None knoweth the harbor as he!)
To lie where the slow tide creeps hither and fro And the
shifting sand laps me around, for I know That my gallant old
crew are in Port long ago -- For ever at peace with the sea!

Quebec 1608 –1908

Of old, like Helen, guerdon of the strong --
Like Helen fair, like Helen light of word, --
"The spoils unto the conquerors belong.
Who winneth me must win me by the sword."

Grown old, like Helen, once the jealous prize
That strong men battled for in savage hate,
Can she look forth with unregretful eyes,
Where sleep Montcalm and Wolfe beside her gate?

Then and Now

Beneath her window in the fragrant night
I half forget how truant years have flown
Since I looked up to see her chamber-light,
Or catch, perchance, her slender shadow thrown
Upon the casement; but the nodding leaves
Sweep lazily across the unlit pane,
And to and fro beneath the shadowy eaves,
Like restless birds, the breath of coming rain
Creeps, lilac-laden, up the village street
When all is still, as if the very trees
Were listening for the coming of her feet
That come no more; yet, lest
I weep, the breeze Sings some
forgotten song of those old years
Until my heart grows far too glad for tears.

Unsolved

Amid my books I lived the hurrying years,
Disdaining kinship with my fellow man;
Alike to me were human smiles and tears,
I cared not whither Earth's great life-stream ran,
Till as I knelt before my mouldered shrine,
God made me look into a woman's eyes;
And I, who thought all earthly wisdom mine,
Knew in a moment that the eternal skies
Were measured but in inches, to the quest
That lay before me in that mystic gaze.

"Surely I have been errant: it is best
That I should tread, with men their human ways."
God took the teacher, ere the task was learned,
And to my lonely books again I turned.

The Hope of My Heart

"Delicta juventutis et ignorantius
ejus, quoesumus ne memineris, Domine."

I left, to earth, a little maiden fair,
With locks of gold, and eyes that shamed the light; I prayed
that God might have her in His care
And sight.

Earth's love was false; her voice, a siren's song; (Sweet
mother-earth was but a lying name)
The path she showed was but the path of wrong And shame.

"Cast her not out!" I cry. God's kind words come --
"Her future is with Me, as was her past;
It shall be My good will to bring her home At last."

Penance

My lover died a century ago,
Her dear heart stricken by my sland'rous breath,
Wherefore the Gods forbade that I should know
The peace of death.

Men pass my grave, and say,
"'Twere well to sleep,
Like such an one, amid the uncaring dead!"
How should they know the vigils that I keep,
The tears I shed?

Upon the grave, I count with lifeless breath,
Each night, each year, the flowers that bloom and die,
Deeming the leaves, that fall to dreamless death,
More blest than I.

'Twas just last year -- I heard two lovers pass
So near, I caught the tender words he said:
To-night the rain-drenched breezes sway the grass
Above his head.

That night full envious of his life was I,
That youth and love should stand at his behest;
To-night, I envy him, that he should lie
At utter rest.

Slumber Songs

I

Sleep, little eyes
That brim with childish tears amid thy play,
Be comforted! No grief of night can weigh
Against the joys that throng thy coming day.

Sleep, little heart!
There is no place in Slumberland for tears:
Life soon enough will bring its chilling fears
And sorrows that will dim the after years.
Sleep, little heart!

II

Ah, little eyes
Dead blossoms of a springtime long ago,
That life's storm crushed and left to lie below
The benediction of the falling snow!

Sleep, little heart

That ceased so long ago its frantic beat!
The years that come and go with silent feet
Have naught to tell save this -- that rest is sweet.
Dear little heart.

The Oldest Drama

"It fell on a day, that he went out to his father to the reapers.
And he said unto his father, My head, my head.
And he said to a lad, Carry him to his mother.
And . . . he sat on her knees till noon,
and then died.
And she went up, and laid him on the bed. . . .
And shut the door upon him and went out."

Immortal story that no mother's heart Ev'n yet can read, nor
feel the biting pain That rent her soul! Immortal not by art
Which makes a long past sorrow sting again

Like grief of yesterday: but since it said
In simplest word the truth which all may see, Where any
mother sobs above her dead
And plays anew the silent tragedy.

Recompense

I saw two sowers in Life's field at morn,
To whom came one in angel guise and said,
"Is it for labour that a man is born?
Lo: I am Ease. Come ye and eat my bread!"
Then gladly one forsook his task undone
And with the Tempter went his slothful way,
The other toiled until the setting sun
With stealing shadows blurred the dusty day.
Ere harvest time, upon earth's peaceful breast

Each laid him down among the unreaping dead.
"Labour hath other recompense than rest,
Else were the toiler like the fool," I said;
"God meteth him not less, but rather more
Because he sowed and others reaped his store."

Mine Host

There stands a hostel by a travelled way;
Life is the road and Death the worthy host;
Each guest he greets, nor ever lacks to say,
"How have ye fared?" They answer him, the most,
"This lodging place is other than we sought;
We had intended farther, but the gloom
Came on apace, and found us ere we thought:
Yet will we lodge. Thou hast abundant room."

Within sit haggard men that speak no word,
No fire gleams their cheerful welcome shed;
No voice of fellowship or strife is heard
But silence of a multitude of dead.
"Naught can I offer ye," quoth Death, "but rest!"
And to his chamber leads each tired guest.

Equality

I saw a King, who spent his life to weave
Into a nation all his great heart thought,
Unsatisfied until he should achieve
The grand ideal that his manhood sought;
Yet as he saw the end within his reach,
Death took the sceptre from his failing hand,
And all men said, "He gave his life to teach
The task of honour to a sordid land!"
Within his gates I saw, through all those years,

One at his humble toil with cheery face,
Whom (being dead) the children, half in tears,
Remembered oft, and missed him from his place.
If he be greater that his people blessed
Than he the children loved, God knoweth best.

Anarchy

I saw a city filled with lust and shame,
Where men, like wolves, slunk through the grim half-light;
And sudden, in the midst of it, there came
One who spoke boldly for the cause of Right.

And speaking, fell before that brutish race
Like some poor wren that shrieking eagles tear,
While brute Dishonour, with her bloodless
face Stood by and smote his lips that moved in prayer.

"Speak not of God! In centuries that word Hath not been
uttered! Our own king are we." And God stretched forth his
finger as He heard And o'er it cast a thousand leagues of sea.

Disarmament

One spake amid the nations, "Let us cease
From darkening with strife the fair World's light,
We who are great in war be great in peace.
No longer let us plead the cause by might."

But from a million British graves took birth
A silent voice -- the million spake as one --
"If ye have righted all the wrongs of earth
Lay by the sword! Its work and ours is done."

The Dead Master

Amid earth's vagrant noises, he caught the note sublime:
To-day around him surges from the silences of Time
A flood of nobler music, like a river deep and broad,
Fit song for heroes gathered in the banquet-hall of God.

The Harvest of the Sea

The earth grows white with harvest; all day long
The sickles gleam, until the darkness weaves
Her web of silence o'er the thankful song
Of reapers bringing home the golden sheaves.

The wave tops whiten on the sea fields drear,
And men go forth at haggard dawn to reap;
But ever 'mid the gleaners' song we hear
The half-hushed sobbing of the hearts that weep.

The Dying of Pere Pierre

"... with two other priests; the same night he died,
and was buried by the shores of the lake that bears his name."
Chronicle.

"Nay, grieve not that ye can no honour give
To these poor bones that presently must be
But carrion; since I have sought to live Upon God's earth,
as He hath guided me,
I shall not lack! Where would ye have me lie?

High heaven is higher than cathedral nave:
Do men paint chancels fairer than the sky?"
Beside the darkened lake they made his grave,
Below the altar of the hills; and night
Swung incense clouds of mist in creeping lines
That twisted through the tree-trunks, where the light
Groped through the arches of the silent pines:
And he, beside the lonely path he trod,
Lay, tombed in splendour, in the House of God.

Eventide

The day is past and the toilers cease;
The land grows dim 'mid the shadows grey,
And hearts are glad, for the dark brings peace
At the close of day.

Each weary toiler, with lingering pace,
As he homeward turns, with the long day done,
Looks out to the west, with the light on his face
Of the setting sun.

Yet some see not (with their sin-dimmed eyes)
The promise of rest in the fading light;
But the clouds loom dark in the angry skies
At the fall of night.

And some see only a golden sky
Where the elms their welcoming arms stretch wide
To the calling rooks, as they homeward fly
At the eventide.

It speaks of peace that comes after strife,
Of the rest He sends to the hearts He tried,
Of the calm that follows the stormiest life --
God's eventide.

Upon Watts' Picture "Sic Transit"

"What I spent I had; what I saved, I lost; what I gave, I have."

But yesterday the tourney, all the eager joy of life,

The waving of the banners, and the rattle of the spears,
The clash of sword and harness, and the madness of the strife; To-night begin the silence and the peace of endless years.

(One sings within.)

But yesterday the glory and the prize,
And best of all, to lay it at her feet,
To find my guerdon in her speaking eyes:
I grudge them not, -- they pass, albeit sweet.

The ring of spears, the winning of the fight,
The careless song, the cup, the love of friends,
The earth in spring -- to live, to feel the light --
'Twas good the while it lasted: here it ends.

Remain the well-wrought deed in honour done,
The dole for Christ's dear sake, the words that fall
In kindliness upon some outcast one, --
They seemed so little: now they are my All.

A Song of Comfort

"Sleep, weary ones, while ye may --
Sleep, oh, sleep!"
Eugene Field.

Thro' May time blossoms, with whisper low,
The soft wind sang to the dead below:
"Think not with regret on the Springtime's song
And the task ye left while your hands were strong.
The song would have ceased when the Spring was past,
And the task that was joyous be weary at last."

To the winter sky when the nights were long
The tree-tops tossed with a ceaseless song:
"Do ye think with regret on the sunny days
And the path ye left, with its untrod ways?
The sun might sink in a storm cloud's frown
And the path grow rough when the night came down."

In the grey twilight of the autumn eves,
It sighed as it sang through the dying leaves:
"Ye think with regret that the world was bright,
That your path was short and your task was light;
The path, though short, was perhaps the best
And the toil was sweet, that it led to rest."

The Shadow of the Cross

At the drowsy dusk when the shadows creep
From the golden west, where the sunbeams sleep,

An angel mused: "Is there good or ill
In the mad world's heart, since on Calvary's hill

'Round the cross a mid-day twilight fell
That darkened earth and o'ershadowed hell?"

Through the streets of a city the angel sped;
Like an open scroll men's hearts he read.

In a monarch's ear his courtiers lied
And humble faces hid hearts of pride.

Men's hate waxed hot, and their hearts grew cold,
As they haggled and fought for the lust of gold.

Despairing, he cried, "After all these years
Is there naught but hatred and strife and tears?"

He found two waifs in an attic bare;
-- A single crust was their meagre fare --

One strove to quiet the other's cries,
And the love-light dawned in her famished eyes

As she kissed the child with a motherly air:
"I don't need mine, you can have my share."

Then the angel knew that the earthly cross
And the sorrow and shame were not wholly loss.

At dawn, when hushed was earth's busy hum
And men looked not for their Christ to come,

From the attic poor to the palace grand,
The King and the beggar went hand in hand.

The Night Cometh

Cometh the night. The wind falls low,
The trees swing slowly to and fro:
Around the church the headstones grey
Cluster, like children strayed away
But found again, and folded so.

No chiding look doth she bestow:
If she is glad, they cannot know;
If ill or well they spend their day, Cometh the night.

Singing or sad, intent they go;
They do not see the shadows grow;
"There yet is time," they lightly say,
"Before our work aside we lay";
Their task is but half-done, and lo!
Cometh the night.

In Due Season

If night should come and find me at my toil,
When all Life's day I had, tho' faintly, wrought,
And shallow furrows, cleft in stony soil
Were all my labour: Shall I count it naught

If only one poor gleaner, weak of hand,
Shall pick a scanty sheaf where I have sown?
"Nay, for of thee the Master doth demand
Thy work: the harvest rests with Him alone."

www.ingramcontent.com/pod-product-compliance
Ingram Content Group UK Ltd.
Pitfield, Milton Keynes, MK11 3LW, UK
UKHW041954190726
13854UKWH00005B/1969

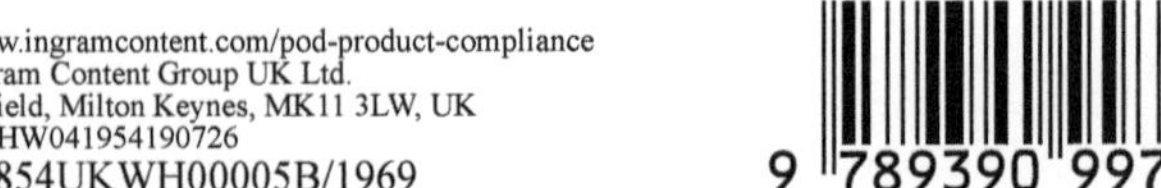

9 789390 997275